Stay Connected
and other Heart-to-Heart Talks

J. P. Vaswani

Other Books by J. P. Vaswani

In English:
10 Commandments of A Successful Marriage
108 Pearls of Practical Wisdom
108 Simple Prayers of A Simple Man
108 Thoughts on Success
114 Thoughts on Love
A Little Book of Life
A Simple and Easy Way to God
A Treasure of Quotes
Around The Camp Fire
Be an Achiever
Be In The Driver's Seat
Begin The Day With God
Bhagavad Gita in a Nutshell
Burn Anger Before Anger Burns You
Dada Answers
Daily Inspiration
Daily Inspiration (Booklet)
Destination Happiness
Dewdrops of Love
Does God Have Favourites?
Formula For Prosperity
Friends Forever
Gateways to Heaven
God In Quest of Man
Good Parenting
How to Overcome Depression
I Am A Sindhi
In 2012 All Will Be Well
India Awake
Joy Peace Pills
Kill Fear Before Fear Kills You
Ladder of Abhyasa
Lessons Life Has Taught Me
Life After Death
Management: Moment by Moment
Mantra for the Modern Man
Mantras for Peace of Mind
Many Paths: One Goal
Many Scriptures: One Wisdom
Nearer, My God, To Thee!
New Education Can Make The World New
Peace or Perish
Positive Power of Thanksgiving
Sadhu Vaswani: His Life And Teachings
Saints for You and Me
Saints With A Difference
Secrets of Health and Happiness
Shake Hands With Life
Short Sketches of Saints Known & Unknown
Sketches of Saints Known & Unknown
Spirituality In Daily Life
Stop Complaining: Start Thanking!
Swallow Irritation Before Irritation Swallows You
Teachers Are Sculptors
Ten Companions of God
The Goal of Life and How to Attain it
The Little Book of Freedom From Stress
The Little Book of Prayer
The Little Book of Service
The Little Book of Success
The Little Book of Wisdom
The Little Book of Yoga
The Magic of Forgiveness
The Miracle of Forgiving
The New Age Diet: Vegetarianism For You And Me
The Perfect Relationship: Guru and Disciple
The Seven Commandments of The Bhagavad Gita
The Terror Within
The Way of Abhyasa (How To Meditate)
Thus Have I Been Taught
Tips For Teenagers
What to do When Difficulties Strike
What You Would Like To Know About Hinduism
What You Would Like To Know About Karma
Why Be Sad?
Why Do Good People Suffer?
Women: Where Would The World Be Without You?
You Are Not Alone God Is With You!
You Can Change Your Life

Story Books:
101 Stories For You And Me
100 Stories You Will Never Forget
25 Stories For Children and Also For Teens
Break The Habit
It's All A Matter of Attitude
Snacks For The Soul
More Snacks For The Soul
The Lord Provides
The Heart of a Mother
The Highway to Happiness
The King of Kings
The One Thing Needful
The Patience of Purna
The Power of Good Deeds
The Power of Thought
Trust Me All in All or Not at All
Whom Do You Love The Most
You Can Make A Difference

In Hindi:
Aalwar Santon Ki Mahaan Gaathaayen
Aapke Karm, Aapka Bhaagya Banaate Hai
Aatmik Jalpaan
Aatmik Poshaan
Bhakton Ki Uljhanon Kaa Saral Upaai
Bhale Logon Ke Saath Buraa Kyon?
Brindaavan Kaa Baalak
Dainik Prernaa
Dar Se Mukti Paayen
Ishwar Tujhe Pranaam
Jiski Jholi Mein Hain Pyaar

Krodh Ko Jalaayen Swayam Ko Nahin
Laghu Kathaayein
Mrutyu Hai Dwar... Phir Kyaa?
Nava Pushp (Bhajans In Hindi and Sindhi)
Praarthna Ki Shakti
Pyar Kaa Masihaa
Sadhu Vaswani: Unkaa Jeevan Aur Shikshaayen
Safal Vivah Ke Dus Rahasya
Santon Ki Leela
Shamsheelta Ka Jaadoo
Srimad Bhagvad Gita: Gagar Ma Sagar

In Sindhi:
Burn Anger Before Anger Burns You
Jaade Pireen Kaare Pandh
Munhinjee Dil Ta Lagee Laahootiyun Saan
Why Do Good People Suffer
Vatan Je Varnan De

In Marathi:
Krodhalaa Shaanth Karaa, Krodhane Ghala Ghalnya Purvee (Burn Anger Before Anger Burns You)
Life After Death
Pilgrim of Love
Sind and the Sindhis
Sufi Sant (Sufi Saints of East and West)
What You Would Like To Know About Karma

In Kannada:
101 Stories For You And Me
Burn Anger Before Anger Burns You
Life After Death
Tips for Teenagers
Why do Good People Suffer

In Telugu:
Burn Anger Before Anger Burns You
Life after Death
What You Would Like To Know About Karma

In Arabic:
Daily Appointment With God
Daily Inspiration

In Chinese:
Daily Appointment With God

In Dutch:
Begin The Day With God

In Bahasa:
A Little Book of Success
A Little Book of Wisdom
Burn Anger Before Anger Burns You
Life After Death

In Spanish:
Aprenda A Controlar Su Ira (Burn Anger Before Anger Burns You)
Bocaditos Para el Alma (Snacks For The Soul)
Dios (Daily Meeting With God)
El Bein Quentu Hagas, Regresa (The Good You Do Returns)
Encontro Diario Con Dios (Daily Appontment With God)
Inicia Tu Dia Con Dios (Begin The Day With God)
L'Inspiration Quotidienne (Daily Inspiration)
Mas Bocaditos Para el Alma (More Snacks For The Soul)
Mata Al Miedo Antes De Que El Miedo Te Mate (Kill Fear Before Fear Kills you)
Queme La Ira Antes Que La Ira Lo Queme A Usted (Burn Anger Before Anger Burns You)
Sita Diario Ku Dios (I Luv U, God!)
Todo Es Cuestion De Actitud! (Its All A Matter of Attitude)
Vida Despues De La Muerte (Life After Death)

In Gujarati:
It's All A Matter of Attitude

In Oriya:
Burn Anger Before Anger Burns You
More Snacks For The Soul
Pilgrim of Love
Snacks For The Soul
Why Do Good People Suffer

In Russian:
What Would You Like To Know About Karma

In Tamil:
10 Commandments of a Successful Marriage
Burn Anger Before Anger Burns You
Daily Appointment with God
Its All A Matter of Attitude
Kill Fear Before Fear Kills You
More Snacks For The Soul
Secrets of Health and Happiness
Snacks For The Soul
Why Do Good People Suffer

In Latvian:
The Magic of Forgiveness

Other Publications:
Recipe Books:
90 Vegetarian Sindhi Recipes
Delicious Vegetarian Recipes
Simply Vegetarian

Books on Dada J. P. Vaswani:
A Pilgrim of Love
Dada J.P. Vaswani: His Life and Teachings
Dada J.P. Vaswani's Historic Visit to Sind
Dost Thou Keep Memory?
How To Embrace Pain
Living Legend
Moments with the Master

STERLING PAPERBACKS
An imprint of
Sterling Publishers (P) Ltd.
Regd. Office: A-59, Okhla Industrial Area, Phase-II,
New Delhi-110020. CIN: U22110PB1964PTC002569
Tel: 26387070, 26386209; Fax: 91-11-26383788
E-mail: mail@sterlingpublishers.com
www.sterlingpublishers.com

Stay Connected and other Heart to Heart Talks
© 2014, J. P. Vaswani
ISBN 978 81 207 8957 9

All rights are reserved.
No part of this publication may be reproduced, stored in a retrieval system or transmitted, in any form or by any means, mechanical, photocopying, recording or otherwise, without prior written permission of the author.

DADA VASWANI BOOKS
Visit us online to purchase books on self improvement, spiritual advancement, meditation and philosophy. Plus audio cassettes, CDs, DVDs, monthly journals and books in Hindi.
www.dadavaswanisbooks.org

Printed in India
Printed and Published by Sterling Publishers Pvt. Ltd.,
New Delhi-110 020.

Contents

Stay Connected	8
The Gift of Tears	17
The Simple Path	25
A Revolutionary Saint	33
The Vision of Sant Kabir	41
Conquer the Ego	49
What the Saints Have in Common	57
Birds of a Feather Flock Together	66
You Can Become New	74
True Inner Freedom	82
When Will India be Truly Free	90
A Love Story With a Difference	98
The Secret of Radha	106
Ten Types of Sin	114
The Easiest Way to God in Kaliyuga	122

God is our friend – the Friend of all friends – the One constant, unchanging Friend. He is available to us all the twenty-four hours of the day and night. He is ever ready to help us. How many of us seek His help?

Stay Connected

God is our true friend, our guardian and our guide. Let us always seek His help, before turning to worldly sources for support.

Over the years, there is one way I have discovered to connect with the Divine, and I believe it has really drawn me closer to the Lord. I would like to share it with you. It is to sit in silence, in the calm and quiet stillness of the night, before you retire to bed, and go over all the events of the last twelve hours. Start anti-clockwise: at 10 pm or 9 pm (which is just past) and recall your actions during the day that is just over.

Ask yourself: What have I done during the day that is just over?

For some of you, the day might involve questions such as the following:

What was the action I did before I retired to my bed? Was I just watching TV? Or was I spending precious free time with the members of my family?

How and where did I eat my meal – seated with the family around the dinner table, or taking my plate to sit in front of the TV?

How did I spend my evening? Slouched over a newspaper, or reading a good book?

In what frame of mind did I leave work? Irritable and exhausted, or with the sense of having accomplished a day's useful activity?

How did I behave with my colleagues at work? Was I annoyed and suspicious about them, or did I appreciate what they did?

How did I treat my subordinates? Was I kind and courteous at all times, or did I use harsh words to criticise them?

In what frame of mind did I enter the office this morning – with the feeling that work is worship, or feeling lousy about my job and my colleagues?

The routine I have given above, is only an indication. You must fill in details of your own daily schedule. Was I kind and loving to the children? Did I attend all my lectures and pay attention to what was being taught? Was I helpful and polite to my customers? How often did I lose my temper? How often did I speak / think harshly? How many people did I refuse to meet?

Think in the reverse direction. You will realise the mistakes you have made, knowingly or unknowingly. Call God, seek His guidance. Ask Him to forgive you; ask Him to help you to forgive yourself. Ask Him to help you become a better person tomorrow; ask Him for the gift of a more worthwhile life tomorrow.

Pray to God, 'O Lord! Forgive me my faults; forgive my mistakes which I have committed in the last 24 hours. Give me the strength to correct them. Dear God, bestow on me the awareness of the true purpose of my life, and the wisdom to improve my *karma* and to do good deeds!'

In today's world of speed and stress, life has become very uncertain. It would be no exaggeration to say that people who leave home in the morning do not always return to their family in the evening. Fatal accidents are increasing, day by day. Fortunes are made and lost on the stock exchange. Cyber fraudsters are looting people's bank accounts from thousands of miles away. Irate mobs attack and fatally wound innocent citizens and hapless passers-by in troubled areas. Reputed companies declare insolvency and hundreds of workers lose their livelihoods overnight. Strange, unknown viruses attack children and old people, and doctors are unable to locate the right remedies to treat them.

Connecting with God can protect you and your family from untold, unheard of troubles like those I have listed above. Should such mishaps occur in your life, God's infinite mercy can guard you from the worst consequences. Therefore, I say to you: seek Him; seek His protection; seek His never-failing support and help! Stay connected with Him at all times!

A few years ago, some devotees of the Sadhu Vaswani Mission were travelling from Bangalore to Pune by road, to participate in the Master's Birthday Celebrations at the Mission Head Quarters. Their car was brand new; the driver was a long-time employee, a faithful retainer of the family who always put safety before speed. The car's music system was playing *Nuri Bhajans*; a picture of Gurudev Sadhu Vaswani occupied a prominent position on the dashboard of the car. The family members were talking about Gurudev Sadhu Vaswani and his teachings. A senior member began to narrate a miraculous change that the Master had brought about in his life. "See, see his eyes," he exclaimed, pointing to the picture of Gurudev Sadhu Vaswani. "That was exactly how he looked at us, with those eyes filled with infinite, loving compassion…"

All of a sudden, the world seemed to be spinning before their eyes. For a moment, all of them were in a state of complete blackout.

A speeding truck, coming from the opposite direction on the wrong side of the road, hit their car head on. The impact of the heavy truck which had been travelling at high speed was so great that their brand new car turned turtle several times and was thrown completely off the road into a thorny thicket. Two of the passengers were thrown out of an open door. Two more were trapped in the back seat. The driver was jammed between the seat and the steering wheel.

The senior member who was seated next to the driver was the first to open his eyes. And he saw exactly what he had been looking at when the car crashed – the loving and compassionate eyes of Gurudev Sadhu Vaswani.

"Gurudeva! Be with us!" he exclaimed. He turned round to look at the back seat; his young daughter and son-in-law were in a state of shock. But they managed to ask him feebly, "Are you alright father? We are OK."

"*Sahib, sahib,*" cried the driver, trying to open his door. "I do not know what has happened. How is everyone? Where is *chhote saab*?"

Someone was desperately trying to open the front door. It was the brother. He managed to open the jammed door and helped them out, one by one. Everyone was badly shaken, but no one was seriously injured! A few scratches and bruises apart, they were all standing somewhat shakily on their own feet. The younger son had in the meanwhile, gone out on the road to stop a passing vehicle and he returned with help. Everyone was safe and sound – although the car was a total wreck!

"My God, my God," cried the young man who had arrived on the scene to help them. "Looking at that car, no one would believe there were any survivors! You people are truly lucky!"

"It's not a matter of luck, brother" said the father, "it's the grace of our Guru. He was with us, watching us, watching over us. He has protected us from harm."

Sri Ramana Maharishi, a great saint, tells us: "God and Guru are not really different: they are identical. He that has earned the grace of the Guru shall undoubtedly be saved and never forsaken."

How true it is that God and the Guru are identical! There is no difference between the two: indeed, the Guru is our visible God. If you establish a link of love with him, he will ensure that God is always with you. Staying connected to the Guru is staying connected to God.

No amount of devotion, no deed of service, no words of tribute from us can match the magnificence of the Guru's grace on us: therefore our ancient *Upanishads* enjoin us to have the same high devotion for the Guru, as we have for God. When we have established our link of love with the Guru, he, in his grace, will link us with God.

Let us realise this truth: by ourselves we can do nothing. As Swami Vivekananda put it so powerfully, without God's grace, we cannot even cross the threshold of our own homes! Our 'effort' and 'ability' cannot even move a leaf.

We are passing through *kaliyuga* – the age of evil. In this *yuga* the easiest way to establish our connection with God is the *Bhakti Marga* – the path of Devotion. *Bhakti yoga* – the way of love, is the most universal and the most direct way to God.

What this path requires is love and faith of the highest order – entreating God, surrendering oneself, seeking His forgiveness for our sins and evil deeds, beseeching His acceptance of our love, addressing Him as mother and father, pleading with Him to cleanse our minds and hearts of the accumulated filth of multiple births. This path is the path of love, for love is not an attribute of God, love is God, and God is Love. By expanding our capacity to love we can get nearer to God. Love for the Lord should become the magnificent obsession of our lives. Awake or asleep, this love should be vibrant and make us cry out, "I love You God, I want to love You more and more. I want to love You more than anything else in the world."

In the great epic of Mahabharata, we are told that Sri Krishna went to Hastinapur as an Ambassador of Peace. His mission was to restore cordiality and peace between Kauravas and Pandavas. Prince Duryodhana assumed that Sri Krishna would stay with him in the royal palace. But that was not to be. Vidura's wife, who was a devotee of Lord Krishna, prayed sincerely to have Him as their guest, in their humble abode.

She called out to Him in prayer, "O Krishna! You are coming to Hastinapur, we will surely get your *darshan*, but how I wish we may offer you our loving hospitality!"

Even as she prayed, she heard the voice of Sri Krishna. She went out running to see Krishna at her doorstep, and welcomed Him whole heartedly. She did not have much by way of cooked food to offer him, so she picked up a few bananas that they had at home, and offered them to the Lord. In her excitement and devotion, we are told, that she peeled the bananas but threw away the fruit and gave Him the banana skins to eat!

Sri Krishna savoured the banana skins, for they were offered out of true devotion. While this was happening, Vidura arrived and was shocked to see Sri Krishna eating banana skins. In utter consternation he said to his wife, "Do you realise what you are doing? You are feeding the Lord with banana skins instead of the fruit!"

But the true devotee that she was, his wife was oblivious to everything!

She went inside to cook food and served it to the Lord. Sri Krishna relished the food as if it were *chappan bhog* – i.e. a delicious banquet of fifty-six varieties of delicacies. When Vidura ate the first morsel of food, he realised that his wife had forgotten to put salt in all of the dishes. He rebuked his wife, "What's wrong with you today? Why is it that you are serving Him, our Lord, saltless food and banana skins?"

Hearing this, Sri Krishna said to him, "Please do not be harsh on your wife. She has offered me the most delicious food I have ever eaten. It is like the divine nectar of the Gods, because it is cooked with pure love."

The mark of true devotion – *bhakti* – is utter humility. Whenever and wherever a *bhakta* calls out to the Lord from the depth of his heart, with an intense yearning, the Lord responds without delay. He appears before the devotee, fulfilling her / his wishes.

To beginners who are overwhelmed by inadequacy and fear at the very idea of walking the spiritual path, the ways of *karma yoga*, *gnana yoga* and *bhakti yoga* seem so exalted as to be virtually inaccessible to them. To such brothers and sisters, I offer the option of what Gurudev Sadhu Vaswani called "the little way" or the *alpa marga*! Believe me, it is one of the easiest, loveliest ways to stay connected!

The way of love is the "little way". It is the way of the little ones, the way which simple folk, such as we are, can tread. It is the way of *bhakti*, devotion, surrender to the Lord, by offering the love of our hearts to every creature that breathes the breath of life. It is the way of longing, deep yearning for the Soul's Beloved. As a miser longs for gold, as a lover longs for his beloved, as a child longs for its mother, even so, said Sri Ramakrishna Paramahansa, must you long for the Lord. The longing of the heart breaks forth into tears. For the little way is the way of silent, unbidden tears. And as Sant Tukaram exclaims: "Blessed are they who have tears in their eyes. The tears of *bhakti* are more precious than the holy waters of the Ganga, Jamuna and Godavari."

God does not demand great things of us. He wants us to walk the little way. All He asks is this: that you do your duty with devotion and dedication. God is pleased with little things, small prayers, small sacrifices, small charity, a little service; a little prayer and devotion, if it is offered in reverence and dedication with love.

To be drenched in love, to lose oneself in love, is to walk, in Gurudev Sadhu Vaswani's meaningful words, the "little way". And to walk the little way, is to become humble as dust, is to be emptied of the self and all that the 'self' stands for – the clamour and confusion of our sordid, selfish, earthly existence.

The Lord has given us the freedom to choose the path that appeals to us, one which suits our temperament and disposition. Let us choose any path, but let us follow it sincerely. By the grace of God, one day, we shall surely reach the goal and our life will be truly blessed!

May I offer you a few practical suggestions to stay connected with God?

1. Begin the day by expressing your love for God; bring your day to a close by expressing your gratitude to God.

2. Everyday, spend some time in silent communion with God; He is not from you afar! He dwells within the Lotus of Your heart.

3. He is also the Indweller, the *antaryami* in every creature that breathes the breath of life. Therefore, treat everyone, every creature, every thing around you with reverence.

4. The Guru is the living, moving image of God. When you love, serve and devote your life to the Guru, you become secure in God's grace.

    Stay Connected — Stay Protected and blessed!

The essential thing in life is to cultivate devotion to God and to have an intense yearning for His Lotus Feet. Nothing else counts.

The Gift of Tears

Have you ever shed tears of love and longing for the Lord? If you haven't, you are still far removed from the bliss, the ecstasy of loving Him.

What do tears have to do with love, some of you may ask.

Have you seen how children cry when their mothers have to leave them for one reason or the other? It is not that they cry because they are unhappy – they cry because they love their mother so much that they cannot bear to be parted from her.

Older children too, shed tears for their mother, when she is suffering or in pain.

A famous Italian Soprano who was a celebrated superstar in her profession, was receiving visitors one evening.

"Now I'm tired," she said to her maid as the last one left. "Do not allow any more visitors to come in."

As a famous singer, she had always regarded it as a duty she owed to her numerous fans and admirers to receive their visits and accept their wishes in person. She spared time for this whenever she could.

But today had been hectic, and she wished to retire to bed early.

"There's only one visitor left Ma'am," said the maid hesitantly. "He's just a little boy in unkempt clothes."

"Alright," sighed the Soprano "send him in!"

A little urchin appeared at the door of the room. "Come on in, my son," she called encouragingly. "Tell me your name!"

"Pierre," the boy murmured, entering the room slowly, afraid to move closer to her.

"Come here," she called "And tell me, what I can do for you."

The boy swallowed hard and big tears rolled down his pale cheeks. "It's my mother," he mumbled. "She's very ill, and we don't have money to pay for her medicine...."

"I don't wish to beg," he stammered. "I have brought a poem that I have written. I thought that if you use it in your programme – I mean, if you could sing .... You could pay me – I mean, give me whatever you wish.... And I will never ever forget your kindness...."

"How clever of you dear!" said the great singer kindly, "Give me your poem.... And don't forget to give me your address too!"

She read the poem and she liked it very much. On the very next day, she sang it at the Opera, and her rendering won a tremendous applause. Directly after the programme she went to Pierre's house and met his mother lovingly. With her she had brought the entire day's collection at the Opera House, which she handed over to young Pierre.

"Your song was just beautiful son!" she said, "I loved it, and everybody loved it. Your tears told me how much you love your mother. Please accept this small payment from me, and give your mother the treatment that she needs!"

We must realise that we, too, are children who have been parted from our Divine Mother. We have become separated from God, our true Beloved. Alas, this is a truth that very few of us are aware of — that we are in a state of separation from the Beloved. When this realisation dawns on us, unbidden tears flow out of our eyes.

Gurudev Sadhu Vaswani often said that the best offering you can make to God is the tears of love and devotion. The gift of tears is what the Lord appreciates the most. We make all kinds of offerings to the Lord. In temples and in churches, people donate money, goods, clothes and food. How many of us offer to Him, the gift of tears?

Most of us are caught up in the entanglements of this world. We are enslaved by what the world has given us – pleasure, possessions, power – so much so that we do not even feel the need for God. How then can we shed tears for Him?

It is only after much wandering that this realisation dawns on man – that he is living a life of separation from God. He begins to feel that his wandering has taken him far away from God – and this realisation brings tears to his eyes.

It is then that he must begin his journey *back* to God, for this is the only journey that will make his life worthwhile. When he embarks on this journey, out of the depths of his heart will arise the cry: "Beloved, take the wanderer home!" and unbidden tears flow out from his eyes.

Tears are a sign of inner yearning. Tears are the melted stuff of the soul. Tears are the rivers longing for the ocean, lovers longing for the Beloved and the devotees yearning for 'yoga' – union with the Infinite.

Recently I met a small child. I asked him, what gift he would like to have? Chocolates, biscuits, toys or fancy clothes? The innocent child, with his radiant eyes, replied, "I want to have a *darshan* of my Shyama!" I was astonished. A small boy, longing to see the face of Sri Krishna is certainly unusual. Perhaps he was an awakened soul who was spiritually alert. But sad to say, such souls are rare to find.

Rabia – she whom we call the Mira of Islam – was once asked, "How do you worship God? Do you wait for God to enter your consciousness and then begin your prayer? Or is it the other way round – you begin your prayer and then God enters your heart?"

Rabia replied, "I do neither of these things. When my eyes are moist, when tears of love and longing flow from my eyes, I see God before me."

For some of us the right feeling, the right state of mind, is more difficult to attain. If our hearts are so hardened that they cannot melt in love and devotion, then let us ask God, beg God to pour His grace on us so that we too can cry out to Him, "Lord, take the wanderer Home!"

I said to you earlier that many of us remain trapped in worldly entanglements and allurements. This is true of every worldly person (*sansari jeev*) – he is intoxicated with the pleasures, possessions and powers of this world. He is intoxicated with worldly love and longing – for *I, Me* and *Mine*. For such a man, wrapped up in his own ego, even scriptural truths and profound sayings are conveniently misrepresented to puff up his vanity!

He must detoxify himself of this *maya* and enter into another kind of intoxication – he must lose himself, nay, drown himself in the intoxication of God's love. Such a one will find himself shedding unbidden tears of love and longing for the true and only Beloved.

There was a woman who lost her husband to cancer. She had adored him, and they had led a happy life together. She had been a happy-go-lucky person, and her husband had thought it his life's mission to fulfil her every whim and fancy. When fate snatched him away, she became a changed person. She forgot how to smile.

"Time will heal all scars," her friends said to her. "You have got to get on with your life. You cannot mourn forever!"

"I will not be able to smile," she told them, "for as long as I live. I shall just exist till my time comes – and I'm praying for that blessed moment to come to me as soon as possible."

She lived a life of loneliness, desolation and despair. For her, life had lost all meaning and purpose.

Months passed. Early one morning, she was awakened by the noise of firecrackers and laughter and celebrations. Startled, she got up from bed and looked out of her window.

She had forgotten all about it – but it was the sacred day of *Deepavali*. People were celebrating the festival of lights with fun and laughter and a happy sense of togetherness.

Her eyes fell on two children – a little boy and a girl – in the street below. Their feet were bare and they were shabbily dressed. They had no firecrackers to play with, but they were watching others and enjoying the fun.

On an impulse, she went down to them and brought them inside her home. She shared breakfast with them and asked them what they were doing all alone on their own on *Deepavali* day. "Where are your parents?" she wanted to know.

"We have no parents," they said to her. "We are orphans," they added, as if to help her understand. She felt a lump rising in her throat. "How do you... who looks after you?" she asked them.

"Our neighbours give us something to eat, whenever they can spare it," the boy explained. "We try not to trouble them. The temple priest gives us *prasad* – and that is how we survive."

As she listened to the children, the wealthy woman forgot her own sorrow and misery. "I too, am an orphan like you," she said to them, through tears. But this time, the tears were not of self-pity; they were tears of fellow-feeling, sympathy and compassion. "I think we should celebrate *Deepavali* together, don't you?"

She took them to a huge department store and bought new clothes for them. The children insisted that she should also have new clothes, and helped her to choose them. She found her spirits lifting, and she urged the children to buy all they wanted – toys, games, eats, whatever took their fancy.

At first the children hesitated, for they had never had such an experience ever before. But because she encouraged them to take everything they wanted, they allowed her to indulge them. How their faces sparkled with joy! How their eyes lit up – reflecting the glow, in the woman's eyes too!

Their joy and laughter stole into her heart, and she forgot her loss and grief. As they laughed and chatted and ate together she realised that life was too precious to be spent in sorrow and misery – it was meant to save those in need.

Tears of compassion, sympathy and sacrifice can cleanse and heal the spirit.

A *sanyasi* sat on the banks of the holy Ganga, meditating quietly. He had chosen a lonely and quiet spot so that he would not be disturbed.

However, his concentration was broken by the sound of sobbing. Disturbed, he opened his eyes to see a woman climbing down the steps to the river, carrying a small bundle in her arms. She was obviously a destitute, for her clothes were ragged and torn. She sobbed even louder, as she waded into the river as far as she could and then let go off the object wrapped in the bundle.

It was her dead child, as the *sanyasi* saw with shock and grief.

Removing the white piece of cloth in which the baby had been wrapped, the woman waded back to the steps, and collapsed on the bank, now weeping uncontrollably.

The *sanyasi* saw it all, and understood at once – the poverty of the woman, the tragedy that had struck her, the helplessness and the terrible grief.

He saw and understood the misery and suffering of the downtrodden and deprived. He decided there and then, that he would take religion to the masses, and serve them through religion.

He was none other than Rishi Dayanand, the founder of the Arya Samaj.

Who was it that said, "If you are depressed, it is time for you to open a service station?" I agree with him one hundred percent. For when you look around you, you see that the world is sad, is broken, is torn with tragedy, is smitten with suffering. Living in such a world, we must help as many as we can to lift the load on the rough road of life.

I love to recall the wonderful words of Gurudev Sadhu Vaswani:

> Did you meet him on the road?
> Did you leave him with the load?

On the long, hard, tough road of life, there are many who go about carrying heavy loads. These loads are not always physical. There are many people who carry in their hearts the terrible burdens of worry, care, anxiety and fear. Lighten their loads! Be a burden-bearer! The day on which we have not helped a brother here, or a sister there, a bird here or an animal there – for birds and animals, too, are God's children and man's younger brothers and sisters in the one family of creation – the day on which we have not helped someone in need is a lost day indeed!

Life fulfils itself in service. There is no joy greater than the joy of those who spend themselves in serving those in suffering and pain.

There are as many ways to
God as are the souls of men
seeking Him. For most of us,
perhaps devotion is the
easiest and the simplest.

The Simple Path

Every saint wishes that his true disciples should develop two qualities – *viveka* and *vairagya*.

Viveka is the power of discrimination that helps us to distinguish between the real and the unreal, between *sat* and *asat*. When we attain *viveka* we will realise that what we have been chasing all our life are shadow-shapes, illusions that will not stay with us forever. *Viveka* will lead us on to *vairagya* – the spirit of dispassionate detachment. For if this earth is a shadow, how can we build upon it? What is there that we can be attached to in this world of transience?

I spoke to you of tears — I meant tears that are born out of *viveka* and *vairagya*. Such tears are like the clean and pure Ganga that fell from Heaven, as a result of Bhagiratha's *tapasya*; this Ganga will purify you, cleanse you and set you in the right frame of mind, in the right attitude for *abhyasa*. Allow the tears to flow therefore; they will cleanse you, they will purify your heart. And you will feel that God is not from you afar. He does not stay on a distant star. He is *here* – He is *now* – He is in the heart within you. You can speak to Him, commune with Him as with a friend or with a member of your own family. Establish contact with Him in silence – and be prepared to LISTEN – for it is in the depths of silence that you will hear His divine voice – not in the clamour and noise of this world.

Everyone is born with a divine spark, an inborn sense of yearning for the Divine. The question is how to kindle this spark and let it grow into a conflagration of soulful yearning.

There are many paths to achieve this, as many as there are people in this world. Therefore Sri Krishna says to Arjuna, 'O Arjuna! All the paths lead to Me! On whatever path you choose to walk towards Me, on that path will I come to meet you!" Let us therefore remember: All the paths are good! All the paths lead Godward. Therefore, let us not criticise any path. To each one his own! For all the paths lead to the same goal, to the Lotus Feet of the Lord.

Our scriptures describe, among others, three such paths. The first path is *Gnana Marga*, the way of True Knowledge. The second path is *Karma Marga*, the way of doing one's Duty. The third path is *Bhakti Marga*, the way of true Devotion.

What is true knowledge? What is the truth? Those who pursue the path of knowledge are in quest of truth. They are in the quest to know God! For as Sri Shankaracharya says, 'God is Truth!'

This world is an illusion (untruth). The man of wisdom, the man of true knowledge in the past, sought to go beyond the gross physical, the merely material; he looked beyond the transient, he was in quest of the 'source', the 'root' the 'ultimate'!

Alas, our quest is different! We have moved away from spirituality. In fact, our society has become 'gross' with over emphasis on food, luxuries and a richly excessive material environment. Everything we value has a price tag attached to it; the more expensive it is, the happier we are to acquire and possess it. We value people and things in terms of money power alone. What is the bank balance of this man? What car is he driving? Where does he live? What kind of clothes is he wearing? We are constantly estimating people's material worth. With such an obsession for the materialistic aspects, how can we even begin to follow the path of knowledge? We are caught up in gross materialism, we have neither the time nor the inclination to search for the Truth, leave alone to find the 'Ultimate'!

The first task a man of knowledge *(Bhramagnani)* sets himself is to detach himself from the gross physical body. He is aware that man is something more – much more than the physical: he is of the spirit, the soul or the inner energy, which gives him life. Today, alas, man is alienated from his spirit; he is so attached to his body, that he keeps pampering it with food, cosmetics and clothes.

Let us accept too, that this body has its needs. The body makes demands on man. Under such conditions, it is difficult to deny it. The realised souls, the Sages and Saints, who have evolved and reached the spiritual ascendency, can say, 'I am not the physical body. I am the immortal soul!' Ordinary human beings, in this materialistic world of *Kaliyuga* are unable to bear witness to this dictum, 'I am That. I am the peaceful Soul. I am *Brahman*, the Ultimate Bliss!'

A young man once said to me: "You often say I am nothing. Haven't you heard of that beautiful, profound dictum, *Aham Brahmasmi*? By saying repeatedly that you are nothing, you insult the *Brahman*. For in reality we are That; we are a Divine Spark of that Infinite Divinity. It would be better, if you said, I am *Brahman*. I am That. *Soham*. Unable to control his anger, he burst out, "I don't think I am nothing! My sense of esteem is far greater than yours. I would not wish to so demean myself as you do."

I smiled and said to him, "If you are indeed the *Brahman*, then why this heated debate? If you are the *Brahman*, then who is the Master, and who is the disciple? Who is the asker and who is to reply? Who are you and who am I?"

This is not to say that the young man was at fault! True it is, that we are Sparks of the Divine. But how can an ordinary man of the world legitimately claim for himself the Divinity of the Eternal Cosmic Soul? The test of this lies, not in proud assertions and grand statements, but in the behaviour of the ordinary man, who lives his life on the earth plane. How does he act, react to events? How does he face adversity and prosperity? For every small mishap, for every small lapse, he bursts into anger. Facing anyone who disagrees with him, or even thinks differently from him, he becomes intolerant and judgemental. Look around you, and you will realise that frustration abounds and the stress and strain of life is visible even on the smiling masks that people 'put on' to face the world.

In short, it is difficult to walk on this path of Knowledge – Truth. Commenting on this path, the great Saint, Sri Ramakrishna Paramahansa, who as we know, actually had the vision of God, said, "I will never say that I am That. I will pray to God, You are my All. You are Supreme. I am but Your humble servant, Your broken instrument."

Would you say that the river is formed from a ripple of water or would you say, a ripple is formed on the river? We are just ripples on the Infinite River. Never make the mistake of thinking yourself to be the Infinite River of bliss. True, you are a spark of Divinity. But you are only a spark, you are not the Ultimate Immortal Supreme Divine Cosmic soul.

Such egotistic thoughts can turn out to be formidable obstacles on this path! By such egoism you are deceiving yourself and those around you! *'Gnana Marga'* is a tough path for the men of *Kaliyuga*, especially if they develop intellectual arrogance.

The second path is *Karma Marga* – the path of rightful action. Do all your actions without expectation or attachment of reward. To perform actions is your duty; but not the right to its rewards. Surrender all your actions to the Lord. It is for the Powers above to grant you the fruit; but you should not expect anything in return for the good actions performed by you!

In the Second Chapter of the Gita, Sri Krishna actually suggests that *Karma Yoga* can help us to get the mind under control, as a requisite step to our proceeding on the path of

Gnana Yoga or the Path of Knowledge. This raises the question: if one is actually competent to walk the path of *gnana*, why should he bother about doing the right type of *karma*?

The answer to this question is that the fruits of *gnana* cannot be realised until one has mastered *karma yoga*. The body, mind and the *antah karna* or inner instrument are all purified by *karma yoga*. All sins are cleansed.

Action, *karma*, is inevitable to human life. Inactivity is physically impossible: even the mere maintenance of the body is not possible without action. Avoiding action does not automatically lead to perfection. What is essential is that we perform right action, avoiding both *akarma* (inaction) and *vikarma* (wrong action).

Karma yoga has been described as the yoga of heroism. It entails that we give up selfishness, which is very difficult to achieve! According to *karma yoga*, spiritual progress begins with selfless service.

Mahatma Gandhi and Albert Schweitzer are two well-known *karma yogis* who walked this path successfully. They spent their life in selfless service of humanity.

The third path is the path of *bhakti*: Gurudev Sadhu Vaswani called this the path of love and longing, the path of devotion, the path of deep yearning!

The Lord, as I said, avers that *Gnana Yoga* is more difficult than *Karma Yoga*. But there is hope for all of us; the path of *bhakti* or devotion is open to us. All it requires is that we focus unswervingly on the Lord – fix our minds on Him, dedicate all our actions to Him and remember Him constantly. If this is not possible, we must serve Him in all our actions. If this too, is difficult, we can simply surrender all our actions to the Lord, renouncing all fruits of action.

May I point out to you, that the twelfth chapter is one of the shortest chapters of the Gita. Sri Krishna chooses to teach Arjuna about *bhakti*, by outlining the qualities of His true *bhakta*.

Thus this chapter becomes a manual of ideal behaviour for those who aspire to true devotion. A true *bhakta*, according to the Lord, regards the suffering of others as his own. He shows no hatred or animosity; he regards none as his enemy. He is unmoved by praise or blame. He is ever ready to help everyone in need. He is aware that service to humanity is service to the Lord Himself. He looks upon joy and sorrow with utter equanimity. Such a devotee is indeed an ideal human being in this imperfect world of ours.

Bhakti yoga – the path of devotion to the Lord – is in essence, the path of love – unconditional, whole-hearted, selfless and completely fulfilling love. Alas, human love is frittered away on worldly objects and goals that are perishable, mortal and therefore, utterly futile. But when our love is directed to God we find complete and absolute fulfilment. We transcend the ego, and commune with the Divine.

May I say to you there are three aspects of *bhakti* – the first is pure love and devotion for the Lord. The true Lover realises, sooner or later, that the goal of his love is complete surrender, nay, complete identification with the Beloved, for this is the end, the aim of true *bhakti*. Surrender is the second aspect of devotion. Then it is that *gnana* dawns on him. Then it is that duality vanishes. Therefore, the *bhakta* claims: "True *gnana* or knowledge is born out of pure love and devotion for the Lord!" This is the third and final aspect.

For those who wish to tread the path of devotion, no scholarship, no rites and rituals are expected! Sant Tukaram and Sri Ramakrishna Paramahansa were not erudite pandits; yet their works are being translated into multiple languages, and research scholars are pouring over their every word to understand their significance and depth!

Alas, we are wrapped up in the veil of worldly emotions. We are away from the vision of the Beauteous face of the Lord! So many veils cover our eyes. Wearing blinkers of darkness we sleep in forgetfulness! Maybe we should keep a whip of thorns to keep us awake and alert!

How may we clean our perception? How may we remove blinkers and see brightness? How may we purify our emotions and behold the Divine? I return to the words of Gurudev Sadhu Vaswani: "Cleanse yourself with the tears of love and longing; wash your sins with the stream of the tears of true repentance."

Draupadi called out to the Lord in utter surrender and devotion; child Dhruva remembered Him with constant *naam smaran* uttered with tears of yearning to attain to His heavenly love; an aged and frail Shabari, washed Sri Rama's feet with her tears of adoration. Mira shed pious tears in the agony of separation from Him.

Love as *bhakti* is intense, selfless and pure. Such love can bring us, face to face, with the Lord. It can destroy all sorrows and sufferings of worldly existence and bring lasting peace and joy into our lives. All of us can aspire to this love! It can be cultivated through *Satsang, Naam Japa, Smaran, Kirtan*, Selfless service of devotees and Study of the scriptures. With or without these *sadhanas, bhakti* can be fostered through tears of yearning and longing for His Lotus Feet!

Tears are valuable. Each tear is precious! Learn the value of tears. Tears can take you into the arms of the Beloved!

How may we know that we are drawing closer to God? The closer we draw to God, the more tender and compassionate become our hearts to the needs of those around us.

A Revolutionary Saint

In one of Sant Kabir's moving *dohas* we have the words:

> In Rama's supreme courts, untruth (falsehood) will be defeated. Those who cross the bar and pass the test, they alone bear witness to Truth!

The Hindi word *kasauti* has a multi-layered meaning: it is a touchstone on which gold is rubbed to ensure that it is pure; *kasauti* also means the criterion or the norm by which something is measured; *kasauti* also means a test or an ordeal. Today we use the word to mean an exam, quiz or challenge. A person in difficulties is said to be facing a *kasauti* so that time will prove whether he comes out shining like real gold or impure gold of no value!

"Gold is tried by touchstone and men by gold," said Francis Bacon four centuries ago. Many of us think that the touchstone method of testing gold came to us from the Greeks; but Kautilya mentions the use of the touchstone to test the purity of gold in his *Arthashastra*, written around the 4th century B.C.

India is considered to be the land of saints and sages. For centuries many saints have taken birth on the sacred soil of India and have influenced the lives of countless number of people. It can truly be said that no other country has been blessed with so many saints. One such saint, was Sant Kabir. In fact, he is regarded by many as a spiritual giant among saints. Some even regard him as a manifestation, an incarnation of God Himself.

Sant Kabir, appeared in the year 1398. Around that time, India was passing through a difficult period of her history. His arrival heralded a new era.

There are different accounts describing his birth.

According to some of them we are told that, one day, a small child was found lying under a tree, sucking his thumb. His eyes shone brightly, and a beatific smile was on his face. Others say that a small child was found atop a lotus leaf in a lake in Banaras. Nobody really knows where and how he was born. Some are even of the opinion that pillars of light descended from Heaven, touched the waters of the lake, and thus, the child was created.

There is only one common ground of agreement that, during his childhood he was brought up in a poor Muslim family. The father's name was Niru, and the mother was Nima. Both Nima and Niru were illiterate and poor and belonged to the underprivileged class. They were childless, and having discovered the abandoned baby, took him home and brought him up as their own child.

A *Kazi* – Muslim priest – was called for the naming ceremony. When the *Kazi* opened the Holy Qur'an the first word spotted by him was Kabir. The *Kazi* closed his eyes, said his prayers and opened the Qur'an again. Again, his gaze fell on the word Kabir. Kabir is a Name of God. How could a child coming from this lowly background, be named after God? The meaning of the word Kabir is the Almighty One, the Highest One. The *Kazi* thought that it was inappropriate for this child to be given this name. So he asked them to wait awhile. Once again, he closed his eyes, offered a prayer and opened the Qur'an Sharif. His eyes fell on the word Akbar. Now Akbar is also another Name of God. Allah-O-Akbar - Allah, the greatest of the Great. The *Kazi* was bewildered. He felt that he could not, should not, give a child of a backward class, a name like Akbar.

In the meantime, Niru and Nima got impatient and did not want to wait anymore. They decided to name their child Kabir.

As a child, Kabir's heart was full of mercy and compassion. On the occasion of *Bakri Id*, as per custom, an animal is bought and sacrificed ritually. The meat is cooked and distributed as holy *prasad*. *Id* was nearing, and Kabir's father said to him, "My child, we shall purchase a lamb and sacrifice it on the day of *Id*."

Kabir exclaimed, "Sacrifice it! What does that mean?"

The father explained, "According to our custom, we buy an animal, bring it home, feed it well and on the day of *Id*, sacrifice the animal. It is slaughtered and cut into pieces and cooked for the feast."

Hearing this, Kabir was horrified. He exclaimed, "Get it home? Feed it well and then slaughter and cut it into pieces? What kind of festivity is this?" It was beyond the child's understanding.

However, Niru brought the lamb and tied it up in the house. From that day, child Kabir was unable to eat a morsel. When food was brought to him, he refused to eat it, for he had lost his appetite. His parents asked him what was his problem? What had happened to him? Without answering, Kabir would go and sit near the lamb and shed tears. He would pat the lamb lovingly and would say, "Now you shall be with us only for a few days. After that, my father, with his own hands, will slaughter you."

The parents found it unbearable to see him crying. They said to him, "Son, you are the light of our eyes, the soul of our being. Why are you crying?"

Kabir said, "I am unable to take in the horror of what I have been told. I am unable to bear it. There is a storm of agony in my heart. This goat which we have kept with us and whom we have been feeding, we are going to slaughter it with our own hands! How can we do such a thing?"

Kabir was heartbroken. He could not partake of any food or drink. He spent sleepless nights. He would sit near the lamb and say, "God who has made me and my parents, the One who has made each and every creature, the same God has also made you. Then how can my father slaughter you? I am not able to understand this cruelty."

At last the father comprehends the great depth of sorrow and agony of his son. He promises him that he will not slaughter the lamb, nor will he sell it to anyone else. The lamb would stay with them as a member of their family. Hearing those words from the lips of his father, Kabir dances with joy. He literally jumps with delight. Was he not an angel of compassion?

Abstain from meat and fish. Treat all creatures with mercy and compassion. This was his teaching to all. He could not bear to see the pain and suffering of others.

One day, Kabir's father said to him, "Today, I am not feeling too well. I have woven the cloth, but will not be able to take it to the market-place."

His mother added, "There is not a grain of food in the house, that is why I would like you to go to the market-place and sell the cloth. You may be young, but you are intelligent and sensible. You are a child blessed with awareness and common sense. I believe, you will be able to sell the cloth, collect the money and buy food grains, so that we may have something to eat today."

Kabir was very pleased and thought to himself, "My father trusts me. I'll go to the market-place and sell the cloth and earn a lot of money and bring home the food grains. Then my parents will be proud of me." With these thoughts in his mind, Kabir was on his way to the market, when he came across an old, feeble person who was shivering with cold and crying out for help. "Is there anybody here to clothe me so that I can cover myself and keep myself warm?" he cried, "I cannot bear this terrible cold." Hearing this painful cry for help, Kabir thought, "I have a full load of cloth, this man requires just a little of it! I shall give him some cloth and sell the remaining at a good price and fulfill the requirements of the family. Father, on seeing the things I bring in exchange, will surely be satisfied. He will not even ask me whether I sold all the cloth or gave a part of it away."

Kabir cut some yards of cloth and spread it over the old and feeble-bodied man. He said to the old man, "Baba, you are like my father. I humbly offer this cloth to you, kindly accept it."

The old, feeble man looked at the attractive face of Kabir and said to him, "My child, there is so much love in your heart! No one has ever spoken to me the way you have done today. I salute you. May God's blessings be showered on you. But, I would like to tell you, back home I have a wife and children, and they too, are shivering in the cold. I'm not asking you for more cloth but I just thought that you should know. You are a small child, I do not want to deprive you further. I just want to convey this information to you."

Kabir's heart was so tender, kind and caring for others, that on hearing what the old man had to say, he forgot his errand and told him, "Take this whole load of cloth with you and protect your wife and children from the cold."

Kabir gave away all the cloth, but later it dawned on him, that he was supposed to bring back home flour, pulses, rice, etc. Where would he procure those from?

He roamed around in the streets for some hours, but being a small child, how long could he remain away from home? Finally, he did come back home. At home, his parents were waiting anxiously for his return. The father thought, "Why did I have to send such a small child to the market? Perhaps, on the way, someone might have grabbed the cloth from him and beaten him up. What have I done? What has become of my dear son?"

When they saw Kabir returning, their eyes shone in hope and happiness. They found his hands empty and felt that, perhaps, the food grains and other articles were being brought by someone who followed him. When Kabir told them of what had happened, they were deeply disappointed and angry with Kabir. But Kabir insisted, "Dear father and mother, believe me, that poor man's need was much greater than our own!"

Gurudev Sadhu Vaswani said to us, "Never forget that the poor and needy, the forsaken and forlorn are pictures of God. To serve them is truly to worship God."

As Kabir grew in years, he kept asking himself, again and again, "What is the purpose for which I have been given this human birth? O Lord, grant me the strength and the wisdom to fulfill this purpose."

It is said that Kashi is the holiest of holy cities, the abode of Vishweshwara, the Lord of the Universe. Then, as now, it was the preferred place for *sadhus* who thronged the city at all times. Those *Sadhus* obviously exercised a profound influence on the life of Kabir. While playing with other children, he would often call *"Rama Rama"* or *"Hari Hari"*. Hindu children playing with him told him not to utter the Name of their Lord – while Muslim children told him not to utter the name of infidels. He would tell them: "Infidels are those who kill the innocent and steal."

When Kabir called on Rama, Hari or Govind, the Muslims were incensed and accused him of being an infidel: when he smeared the sacred ash or put a *tilak* on his forehead, the Hindus told him angrily not to misuse the symbols of their religion.

Kabir was in search of a Guru, who would guide him. When our thirsty hearts yearn for God, then the need for a Guru arises – a Guru who may hold our hand and lead us on – ever onward, forward, Godward!

In the heart of Sant Kabir, was the deep longing to find a Guru. He saw people visiting temples and mosques, bathing in holy waters, fasting, performing rituals and he thought: "I desire to go on a pilgrimage within, for which I need the guidance of a true Guru."

I will tell you how Kabir found his Guru, with the grace of God!

The human soul is a spark of the Universal Spirit or God as we call Him. When we live our daily life in the realisation of this truth, the body becomes a temple that is worthy to be inhabited by the Spirit! Discover God within you.

The Vision of Sant Kabir

I was telling you about Kabir's yearning to find his Guru.

Who is a Guru? A Guru is one who has not merely studied the Vedas and the Scriptures or one who reads a few books and gives discourses. A Guru is essentially a man of experience, of God-realisation. A true Guru is a friend of God. He walks with God. He talks to God. He lives and moves and has a perpetual fellowship with God. His every moment is spent in the presence of God. There is no difference, no separation, between such a person and God. To see such a one, is to see God Himself. Even if we were to go and meditate in the forest for several years, face hardships and practise austerities, or if we were to undertake a vow of silence or fast for years, or go on pilgrimages; it is nothing compared to spending a short time in the company of a true Guru!

To light a candle, you require another one that is already lit, or a matchstick. Similarly, to be able to kindle the light within, you require the company of a person who is already illumined. The Guru is an illumined soul; it is only he who can help enlighten another soul.

Kabir's quest took him to many a Muslim priest, but he saw that their lives were a facade. They read the Holy Qur'an, but there was no love for truth in their lives: they were prejudiced and differentiated between friends and enemies. They called the Hindus *kafirs*, infidels, and showed no mercy and kindness towards birds and animals. Like many common men, they lamented in sorrow and exulted in joy. They could not be true Gurus! He said to himself, "I need a Guru who will lead me to the Lotus Feet of God."

As for the Brahmin pandits, they were steeped in bigotry, arrogance of birth and empty spiritualism. They taunted Kabir on account of his low birth, and hurled abuses at his ignorance.

He prayed to God: "O Lord, You have not sent me to this earth-plane to waste my life in vain, by frittering it away in pursuit of pleasures. You have given me this human birth to become one with You. Bring me into contact with a realised soul who can lead me to You."

In those days there was a great saint named Ramanand. Kabir wanted to make Ramanand his Guru, but Ramanand, in the interest of peace among communities, was not prepared to accept a Muslim as his disciple. However, Kabir was determined to have Ramanand as his Guru. He learnt that Ramanand began his day by taking a dip in the sacred Ganges at four in the morning, after which he would sit for his daily prayers.

One day, Kabir awoke before four in the morning and lay down on one of the steps that led to the river bank. Sant Ramanand, as was his daily routine, proceeded to the river in the dark of the dawn, chanting the Name of Rama. As he went down the steps that led to the river, suddenly his feet touched the body of a man lying on the steps. He exclaimed loudly, "Rama, Rama, Rama".

On hearing the words, "Rama, Rama, Rama", Kabir immediately got up and clapped his hands in the joy of having found a Guru and received the *Guru mantra*. "I have received what I intensely longed for," he exclaimed.

From that day onwards, Kabir started telling everyone, "Sant Ramanand is my Guru and, in his mercy, he has given me a *Guru-mantra*."

When Ramanand learnt of this, he sent for Kabir and said to him, "I have never accepted you as my disciple. Nor do I remember having given you a *mantra!*"

Kabir reminded him of the incident that had happened a few days earlier, saying, "Gurudev, when you trampled over my body, I held your feet in my hands and you uttered Rama, Rama, Rama, which I took as my *Guru-mantra.*"

Sant Ramanand did remember the incident and became speechless. He could not contradict Kabir. He smiled and said to Kabir, "My child, you win – and I lose!"

Kabir was happy, he had found a true Guru. And he boldly declared that he was a child of both Rama and Allah. He propagated the truth that God is One, though He is called by many Names. Kabir's ecstasy in finding the *Naam* is expressed as the annihilation of his lower self, the ego:

Jab Mein Tha Tab Hari Nahin, Ab Hari Hai Mein Nahin,

Sab Andhiyara Mit Gaya, Jab Deepak Dekhya Mahin

When "I" was, Hari wasn't; now Hari is, and I am not: All darkness was dispelled, when I saw the light within!

One day, as was the custom, Ramanand had a *puja* performed for his ancestors. The *puja* included feeding crows and animals. Rice and other foods were cooked specially for the purpose. Ramanand asked that the food should be spread on the ground for the birds to come and eat it, so that it would reach the ancestors. At this, Kabir remarked that the food would be eaten by the crows, and would not reach the ancestors at all. It dawned on Ramanand, that what Kabir said was, indeed, the truth. After this incident, Ramanand became more liberal in his thinking and realised that many customs were no better than superstitions.

In the days of Sant Kabir, people would go to the forest to meditate, and because of this they would be regarded as saintly souls. Sant Kabir explained to the people, that instead of going to the forest, one needed to go deep within oneself.

Be in the world, but be not worldly, taught Kabir. Therefore, grow in the inner spirit of detachment. Do your duties, fulfill your obligations, but all the time let the thought of God be in the background of your consciousness. The disease from which most of us suffer is the disease of forgetfulness. The mind always keeps on wandering and we keep on wandering with the mind.

This wandering is the root cause of our unhappiness. If only our minds are fixed on God, all our unhappiness would vanish as mist before the morning sun.

Kabir always thought of God as the Formless One and did not believe in idol worship. He said, "The Lord is seated in everyone's heart. Everyone can speak to Him and can hear Him speak. God does not dwell on a distant star. He is wherever we are. He is here, He is now. God can be felt, He can be touched. And, instead of going to temples and so-called holy places, one should enter on the interior pilgrimage."

Hindu *Pandits* said that Kabir was anti-religious, while Muslim *Maulvis* declared him a *kafir* because he did not follow Islam despite being brought up as a Muslim.

Kabir boldly proclaimed that Rama was present in his house, and that he had no need to go to the temple and mosque; he told everyone to seek Rama and Rahim, Keshav and Kareem in their own hearts. For good measure, he added that pilgrimage to Kashi and Kaaba, Dwaraka and Mecca was a waste of time.

It is said that the leading Hindu *Pandits* as well as the powerful *kazis* of his day went to Emperor Sikander Lodhi to launch a complaint against him: as a Muslim who had put on a sacred thread, he was a threat to both Islam and Hindu faith! The emperor listened to the religious leaders, and called for Sant Kabir. Kabir arrived at the *darbar* long after the summons were sent.

The emperor was very angry and asked Kabir, "How is it that you have delayed answering the royal summons?"

Kabir smiled and said, "I was absorbed by an engaging spectacle that I could not leave off watching."

"And what was that engaging spectacle?"

"I saw thousands upon thousands of camels and elephants passing through a hole smaller than the eye of a needle."

"Kabir, you lie!" said the emperor, very angry now.

Kabir was unfazed. "O, Shah, see for yourself how far away are the sun and moon and stars from this earth: in the vast spaces between them, how many camels and elephants roam? And do we not perceive them all, the sun, the moon, the stars, the camels and the elephants through the pupils of our eyes? Is not the pupil of an eye smaller than the needle?"

The Emperor was astounded by this answer. However, he said to Kabir, "I hear that you persist in telling the people to utter the name of Rama. Is this not against the tenets of Islam?"

To this accusation Kabir is said to have replied:

Ram Rahim, Karim Are One; Allah And Satnam Are One;
Bismillah And Bhishamwar Are One; Truth Is One. God Is One.

The Emperor was so impressed by Kabir's wise words that he too, wanted to become Kabir's disciple. To this Kabir replied, *"Das* Kabir says, choose your own path! Let everyone choose their own path!"

Saints do not force anyone to follow a particular faith. A true saint allows his disciple to choose his own faith, and follow his own path.

What matters is your inner purity – your inner life! Outwardly, you may follow any faith, but the inner life must be a life of love, devotion, and detachment.

Kabir too tried to explain to the Emperor, that whatever one's faith, it is the inner purity which is the true religion of man. Everyone on the earth breathes the same air. Be he Hindu or Muslim, everyone inhales the same energy, and lives by the same energy.

He told the Emperor and his *kazis*: "You are Mussalmans, so be true Mussalmans!" To the Hindu *pandits* he said, "You are Hindus, so be true Hindus! Whatever faith you are born in, live it and be faithful to it. Hindus, Muslims are the children of the same father – call him Allah, the merciful or Rama the Ideal or Hari the Protector. These are different names of the One Supreme Being."

Kabir's religious views did not go well with the *kazis*. They ordered the guards at the palace to imprison him. He had failed Islam. He was a slur on their religion.

Kabir remained calm inside the prison. He was lost in singing the sacred *naam* of Sri Rama.

This annoyed the chief *kazi* so much that he ordered Kabir to be released and to be trampled by a wild elephant. The guards released Kabir and brought him out into the yard. The *kazis* said to him: "Give up your chant of Sri Rama or else we will have you trampled and crushed to death in a moment."

Kabir remained undaunted. He refused to give up chanting the sacred name of Sri Rama. The *kazi* too was adamant. The guards brought in the elephant and lo and behold, a miracle happened. The wild elephant walked gently towards Kabir, bowed to him and went away!

The *kazi* was wonder struck. "Tell us the secret of the wild elephant's reverence for you. Why did he not trample you?"

To this Kabir replied:

Kabir says, Gobind is Everywhere
He is Near, I Have No Fear.
Gobind Is My Protector; He Is Everywhere!

The Emperor realised that Kabir was a true saint of God, and ordered him to be released immediately.

Gradually, the influence of Kabir grew from more to more. Kabir's discourses attracted many seekers. Everyday, more and more people gathered to listen to him.

Kabir sang many a song. His language and style were simple and direct. Though centuries have passed, Kabir's songs and *slokas* continue to be sung in numerous homes and temples, with fervour and devotion.

Sant Kabir continued to live in Kashi. On the opposite bank of the sacred river Ganga was a small town called Maghar. It was believed that whosoever breathed his last in Kashi would reach the gates of Heaven, and whosoever passed away in Maghar, would go to Hell. To educate the people, Kabir asked his followers to take him to Maghar, where he breathed his last.

When Kabir died, his body was claimed by both Hindus and Muslims. The Hindu followers wished to cremate the body, the Muslim followers wished to bury it. There is a story which tells us that while the Hindus and Muslims were engaged in a dispute, a little child lifted the shroud – and found that the body was gone! Instead there was a heap of flowers.

Truly, Kabir lived like a flower. Wherever he went, he spread the fragrance of his love-filled life. His teaching can be summed up in two words: Detach – Attach. Detach yourself from the world – its pelf, pleasure, power: and attach yourself to the Lotus Feet of the Lord – where alone is love, joy and peace. Let us live in the world – but let us not allow the world to live within us. Or, as Sri Ramakrishna often said, "Let the boat float over the waters but, let not water enter the boat."

Is this not the true touchstone of the realised soul?

> When the ego goes, the light
> of God glows!

Conquer the Ego

In one of the Sikh Scriptures, we have the following words:
Sagal Purakh Mein Purakh Pradhan
Saadh Sangi Ja Ka Mitey Abhimaan
What mean those words?

Among all persons, the noblest is even he who gives up his egotistical pride in the company of the Holy.

Who, living in the company of the Holy, renounces all pride. He becomes humble as ashes and dust.

Through these words Guru Arjan describes the noblest person, the perfect person: who is he?

If we try to answer that question by worldly standards, we would think of the mighty, the powerful, the rich, the famous, the celebrities such as Hollywood and Bollywood stars. Athletes, film stars, politicians, businessmen, industrialists and VIPs would probably come to our minds. But Guru Arjan has different criteria to choose his perfect man. Who is he? Not the one who wields the most power; not the one who is the most learned; not the one who has accumulated the maximum wealth; nor even the one who has attained the *ashta siddhis* (eight yogic powers) as they are called.

The perfect man is the one who has annihilated the ego. Such a man has attained wisdom and in the knowledge of Truth he has erased his ego. Such a man is the noblest man; such a man is the perfect man; such a man is close to God! He acknowledges the source of his being at every step of his life. Such a man is supreme among all the men in the world.

In the Gita, the Lord says to His dear, devoted disciple Arjuna: "Whatever you do, whatever you give in charity, whatever austerity you practise, do it as an offering unto Me!" This is true *yagna* – to make of your entire life, an offering to the Lord. Sacrifice your ego-self; sacrifice your desire – and do whatever you do for the love of God.

Whatever you do – do it for the love of God. Make your entire life an offering unto God; and when you arrive at this stage, you will find that there is but one aspiration in your heart – you ask for nothing, neither power, nor possessions. The one aspiration of your heart is: unto Thee be all the glory O Lord! Not mine, but Thine be the glory O Lord!

When people attain to levels of true greatness, they view the world from a different perspective altogether. They are unaffected by petty ego clashes; questions of 'big' and 'small' tasks do not affect them.

When America was fighting for its independence under the overall military command of General George Washington, he came across a platoon of soldiers who were trying to shift a huge fallen tree-trunk from one place to another. The tree-trunk was blocking the road and had to be cleared urgently, to allow the free movement of troops.

The Corporal was ordering the soldiers rudely. "Heave, heave!" he shouted. "Get going! Push with all your might!" And again, "Is that your best? Well, it's pathetic!"

Washington was in civilian clothes and no one recognised their distinguished General. Gently, he said to the shouting officer, "Don't you think you should give them a helping hand so that they can do their job better, instead of simply ordering them about?"

"Give them a helping hand?" sneered the man. "You don't know what you're talking about! For your information, I'm a Corporal. These soldiers work *under* me, and it's beneath my dignity to do their job!"

"Alright Sir," said the Chief Commander to the lowest ranking official in his army. "I will offer my help to your men."

He took off his overcoat and joined the soldiers. Not only did he encourage them with words, he also pushed and heaved with them until the tree-trunk was pushed aside and the road was cleared.

When the job was done, he turned to the arrogant Corporal, "Whenever you find your men unable to do a job, please send for me. I will come and give them a helping hand." So saying, he gave the Corporal his card. The Corporal read the card and was immediately flabbergasted. He did not know that the man who stood in front of him was the Chief Commander of the Army.

Have you seen a stagnant pond that has no outlet and does not flow into a canal or stream? Its waters become stale, dirty and covered with thick moss; it begins to smell bad; it becomes the habitat of frogs. So it happens with a life that does not flow out through good deeds performed for others' benefit; it too becomes stale and stagnant with vanity, ego, selfishness and desire. But a life that is spent in the service of others, flows clean and free like a sparkling river and ultimately reaches the ocean of the Supreme Self. Thus, doing good to others, serving others, always turns out to be the best that one can do for oneself!

Cultivate the soul through service! In other words, become aware that you are only an instrument of God. He is the One Worker – you are but His tool, His agent. Therefore, renounce all idea of egoism, of the narrow self and become an instrument of the eternal *shakti* that shapes the lives of individuals and nations.

It is good that those who seek to serve others bear this in mind: that service is meant to purify the mind, heart and intellect, and to move us on the path of God-realisation. They are also blessed with the unique, selfless joy that comes from serving those in affliction, and bringing the light of love into dark, unhappy lives. These are the genuine feelings to be nourished by those who save others – and not vanity, ego and self-seeking pride.

Let me appeal to you: do not seek to serve others to prove your superiority. This brings disgrace to you and it degrades those whom you seek to 'serve'. It destroys the very spirit and concept of service. True service is free from the contamination of the ego. Therefore, Gurudev Sadhu Vaswani said to us, "He is great who greatly serves!"

Once, we put a question to Gurudev Sadhu Vaswani: what is true knowledge, absolute knowledge, the greatest wisdom? Gurudev Sadhu Vaswani replied, "True knowledge is the realisation that I am nothing, He is everything. This realisation makes man humble and gentle. And there is no wisdom greater than this."

Gnana (true wisdom) is not gathered from books, but from inner life. This our ancient *rishis* cultivated, and the Guru is one who can impart to us – not merely the text, not merely the 'sayings' and words – but the distilled essence of that wisdom. To be worthy of absorbing that wisdom, a true disciple, a true *shishya*, must be truly humble!

Let me share with you the story of a learned man who sought out a spiritual teacher. He felt he had accumulated enough and more knowledge of all else, and all that remained to make him complete, perfect, in every respect was spiritual knowledge. So he said to the master, "Guruji, accept me as your disciple: and let me begin by telling you all that I have learnt."

And promptly, without waiting for the Guru to respond to him, the man began to list all the subjects he had studied;

the scriptures he had read; the *sadhanas* he had practised. The 'recital' went on and on, and the Guru listened to him in utter silence.

When the disciple had come to the end of his catalogue of learning, the Guru asked him gently, "Would you like a cup of tea?"

"A cup of tea would, indeed, be very welcome," said the man, clearing his parched throat, exhausted by his own eloquence.

The tea was brought. With his own hands, the Guru began to pour the hot tea from the teapot. He poured the golden liquid into a delicate cup, which was soon full to the brim. And still, the Guru continued to pour the tea. The cup overflowed, and the liquid spilt on to the saucer – and still, the Guru did not stop pouring the tea. The tea overflowed on to the tray, the table cloth, and thence on to the floor.

"Stop! Stop!" cried the learned man. "What are you doing? Can't you see that the cup is overflowing?"

"This is what you want me to do," said the master. "Your cup of knowledge is already overflowing. How do you expect me to add anything more to it?"

The Guru is not like a lecturer or professor, who specialises in chalk-and-talk preaching. He is not one who has culled his knowledge and wisdom from books and passes them on to his disciples in capsule form. He is one who has perceived the Truth, seen Reality, and knows from his own life and experience, the way that leads one to that Truth, that Reality.

Some of us consider ourselves so well read, so well informed, that we even sit in judgement on the Guru's words. We analyse and criticise his statements; we compare his teachings to others' views and evaluate them.

In the Veil of Dawn is a beautiful book written by our master, Gurudev Sadhu Vaswani. In this book he reveals one of the secrets of spiritual life. The secret is to have absolute and unquestioning faith in your Guru. Do not ever judge the Guru's actions, do not ever criticise him, the master urges us. If your mind is incapable of such faith and you are threatened by doubts and misgivings, then remind yourself that your Guru at least deserves the respect you would give to a broom. A broom by itself may not be clean, but it sweeps the house clean. Similarly, the Guru, irrespective of his stature, helps to clean our mind. This may sound harsh to some of you; but there are people who constantly ask questions and raise doubts about the Guru's intentions, especially if the Guru thinks differently from them. Therefore, let me say to you, bow down to your Guru in all humility and seek his blessings. This is one of the secrets of the spiritual life, the life of the spirit.

Once upon a time, a man sent his two sons to an *ashram* of saints. His dearest wish was to give them true education. The sons returned home after spending many years in the *ashram*. The father embraced them affectionately and said to them, "My dear sons, welcome back to your family. Go and rest a while; refresh yourselves. When you are rested and relaxed, come and meet me. I would like to have a dialogue with you."

The sons did as they were told. After a comfortable rest and a meal, they sat down to talk to their father. The father asked them eagerly, "My dear sons, tell me what have you learnt from the Gurus in the *ashram?*"

The elder son was very proud and egotistical. He mockingly said, "Father, it is impossible to tell you all that I have learnt. I have delved deep into the ocean of knowledge. I feel that my third eye is opened. I do not know from where to start and where to end. For, the knowledge I have gathered is immense and the experiences I have had are infinite. I doubt very much if you can even begin to grasp the extent of my learning."

Is this not typical of many of us? Human beings are much given to self-congratulations on the least pretext. Every little success or achievement is enough to boost our ego. "I have accomplished that!" "I succeeded in doing this!" we boast, all too often.

The father then turned to the younger son and asked him, "What have you learnt during your stay in the *ashram*?" The young man remained silent, his head bowed down in deep thought. After much cajoling he said, "Father, it is true that my Gurudev has taught me many valuable lessons. But, sitting at his lotus feet I came to realise that all the knowledge I gained from him was not enough and that I had to learn much more from him. On hindsight, I feel that I haven't learnt much. What I have learnt is only a small drop of the vast ocean of knowledge."

Hearing this, the father was very happy. He said, "My dear son, I am happy to know that the years you spent at the lotus feet of your Guru were not wasted. I think you have acquired true knowledge."

Humility and devotion are the signs of true knowledge. Gurudev Sadhu Vaswani, has said, "At the Highest Stage, man is without self."

Humility is a royal quality. There is an indefinable sense of dignity about every truly humble person. Such a one lives in others: the others are in him.

What the Saints Have in Common

Gurudev Sadhu Vaswani was one of the humblest of men that ever trod the earth. In one of his moving poems, he says:

What am I?
A tiny candle:
The flame is Thine!

What am I?
A singing bird:
The song is Thine!

What am I?
A little flute:
The music is Thine!

What am I?
A little flower:
The fragrance is Thine!

What am I?
An earthen lamp:
The light is Thine!

Gurudev Sadhu Vaswani often said, "I am not even a speck of dust. I am a zero – not an English zero, but a Sindhi Zero, which is just a point, a dot." Such was the humility of this great man. Let us introspect and find out what we think of ourselves. Would we ever think that we are nothing? Would we ever consider ourselves the dot which is invisible? Something tells me that for many of us, the answer must be in the negative. We are egoistic. We have a larger than life ego. It is this ego which makes a few of us even go so far as to deny God.

Gurudev Sadhu Vaswani was a man of great scholarship. He had a large private library. I have yet to see such a vast collection of books in a private library. Let me hasten to add, they were not just for display; he had read the books stocked in his library. Apart from the Sindhi and Sufi masters whom he loved, he could refer at will to German mystics like Goethe and Meister Eckhart; he was familiar with the views of Schopenhauer and Nietzsche; he had read Marx and Ruskin, Carlyle and Emerson. He had studied them carefully. His knowledge was vast. He had the knowledge of physical sciences, of politics and economics, sociology and psychology; he was also a man of literature. He had studied history and philosophy and taught it as well at famous colleges. But, he never ever put his deep knowledge on deliberate display, as some men are wont to do! He had the deeper knowledge, the inner wisdom which made him truly humble; so humble that his every action was a loving offering to the Lord!

Today, any man with a little smattering of knowledge thinks himself to be someone extraordinary. Many intellectuals and scholars came to Gurudev Sadhu Vaswani to discuss about truth, knowledge and wisdom. Gurudev Sadhu Vaswani heard their views silently, without interrupting them to put forth his point of view. Some of them would try to provoke him into an argument. Smiling, he would say to them, "It takes two to make a discussion." He often advised us to remain away from discussions. If one person speaks, the other should keep quiet. Those who walk the spiritual path should not indulge in unnecessary debates.

We waste our energy in unnecessary discussions and debates. In such discussions there is always a person with an egoistic bend of mind, whose sole purpose is in challenging and debating to win his argument. Such futile activities take us away from the truth and absolute knowledge. A man of true knowledge knows that he is nothing and all that he has, intelligence, knowledge, intellect, even the ability to express himself forcefully, are all given to him by the Almighty God. This realisation is true knowledge. He is linked with God. He becomes an instrument of God. Such a man is a beacon of light for others. That is one of the reasons that Gurudev urged us to be humble.

Once a young man asked Gurudev Sadhu Vaswani, "Why should we be humble?" It was night and the sky was spangled with stars. Gurudev Sadhu Vaswani gazed at the sky and said, "My dear one, look at the sky and the millions of stars shining above you. Each star has its own universe. In such a vast galaxy of universes this planet earth is merely a speck of dust. And you are a tiny speck upon that speck of earth. Then, why are you proud?"

The young man was not willing to give up. He replied, "I am a human being. Nothing is impossible for me to achieve." Gurudev said, "My dear one, man is nothing, do not be proud. You are just a guest for a short while here upon God's earth."

During his European tour, Gurudev Sadhu Vaswani visited Paris. There he was taken to see the grave of Napoleon the Great. Napoleon was a great General, who became the de facto 'emperor' of France and he had conquered many nations. Gurudev Sadhu Vaswani said later, "When I stood by the grave of this great soldier, my eyes shed tears. The ruler of the great empire was just a fistful of dust. O man, do not be proud, one day you too will be just a fistful of dust."

Gurudev often said to us, "The 'h' of humility is humiliation." If anyone criticises you, if anyone degrades you, if anyone hurts you, then consider yourself to be lucky. Accept the harsh words of criticism and the humiliation, because he lightens the burden of your ego."

Some Gurus, while initiating the disciple give the *mantra*, *'Soham'*. I am afraid some of us misinterpret this powerful word very egotistically! *'Soham'* means 'I am that'. It is a Vedantic dictum. But its meaning is profound, not literal. It refers to the symbiotic unity of "All that is". But when you recite it without the awareness of this unity of all life it only boosts the ego. Gurudev Sadhu Vaswani warned us about the regular incantation of the sacred *mantra, 'Soham',* because, *'Soham' mantra* contains the 'I' i.e. 'I am that '. 'I' is ego. 'I' is the lower self.

Without true knowledge the 'I' (ego) is identified with the Supreme. The 'I' is not the Supreme. It is not what He is. The 'I' is merely a spark of the Divine. It is sad, that the *mantra* 'I am that' is misunderstood and 'I' is identified with God! This *mantra*, as said earlier, seemingly identifies man with God. By constant chanting of this *mantra, 'Soham'*, the ignorant man begins to think that 'he is God'. He is the Supreme Being. His ego reaches the zenith. This ego ultimately brings his downfall. That is why, Gurudev Sadhu Vaswani cautioned us against the chant of *'Soham'*. He preferred the incantation of *mantra 'OM'*.

Very often, the scholars and *pandits* of *Vedanta* are filled with pride; they are filled with ego; they think that they actually know God. How unfortunate this is! Humility which is the true hall mark of wisdom is often lacking in such people.

I recall here the visit of a great *pandit* from north India. He had come to meet Gurudev Sadhu Vaswani. Very proudly he said to Gurudev: "What kind of spirituality are you preaching? You teach, I am nothing. That is not true. I am That! I am That which is! How can man be nothing when he is 'That', when he is 'God'! Our scriptures say, and rightly so: That are Thou! 'I am That'! – *Tat twam asi! Aham Brahmasmi!"*

He proudly went on putting forth his argument. Gurudev Sadhu Vaswani heard him in silence. Without entering into argument with him, he said, "You obviously have views that are very different from mine; I respect your right to hold these views; but my Guru has taught me to be humble as dust and ashes; to serve people in humility. My Guru has taught me that 'I am nothing, He is everything'."

A very interesting story is related in the sequel to the *Mahabharata*. The Kurukshetra war was over and Sri Krishna had departed the earth. Arjuna was travelling across a strange country when he was attacked by robbers.

Now Arjuna was a fearless warrior, and had been the leading light of the Pandava forces in winning the war. Further, his weapons were all divine gifts. Therefore, he fought valiantly against his attackers – but it was to no avail. He was beaten and robbed.

Miserable and despondent, he sought out Sage Ved Vyas and begged him to explain the inexplicable – how was it that he, the invincible Arjuna with his incomparable valour and weapons, faced defeat at the hands of a few ruffians?

Ved Vyas explained to him that neither he, nor his weapons had possessed any intrinsic power. "Your invincibility came from the presence of the Lord who was your Divine Charioteer. It was His power too, that infused your weapons with their might. Now that He is no longer with you, these weapons are useless. And you fight now on your own feeble strength."

Arjuna's eyes were opened to a great truth. Man achieves all that he does only through the sanction and grace of the Divine Will!

We are only too apt to regard our cleverness, our skill, our diplomacy, our tact and our efficiency as the sole reason for our success. A little reflection will make us realise that it is the Divine presence that guides us at every step. Therefore, success and accomplishment should teach us humility instead of pride, and prompt us to express our gratitude to God.

The great German scholar, Reumer, devoted his life to making a thorough study of the lives of great saints. After long and deep study, he observed that these holy men came from very different backgrounds. A few were born wealthy; others were poor; some of them were wise and learned, while a few were not much educated. But without exception, they all had one thing in common – they were men and women of utter humility. This is the distinguishing mark of the genuine saint, the true *fakir* – he is humble.

You may come across many who are wise and learned; they may deliver grand discourses; they may write profound works; they may give brilliant interpretations of the sacred texts. But if they have not conquered their pride, they have not attained sainthood.

St. Francis of Assisi was a gem of the purest ray serene. A group of his detractors once accosted him "Why is it that the world is running after you," they sneered. "You are nothing; you have nothing; you are far from handsome; nobody would give you a second look. You are a pauper and have nothing to give. Your clothes are tattered and your feet are muddy and covered with dust. Why then do people run after you?"

Such was the utter humility of this great saint that he said to them: "My dear brothers! God set out in quest of the most wretched and most lowly among men, so that He could show to the world what His grace could achieve. He looked everywhere and in the whole wide world, He could not find one more wretched than I!"

"The Lord chose to touch this unworthy self with His grace," continued the saint. "I am nothing; whatever I am is thanks to the grace of the Lord."

People often ask me which was the way recommended to us by my beloved Gurudev, Sadhu Vaswani, to attain to the Lord. I tell them: "He taught us to walk the little way."

"Little way!" they exclaim. "What can that be? We have heard of other paths that lead us onward – *bhakti marg, gnana marg, karma marg, hathayog, rajayog* and so on. But never have we come across the little way as you call it. Please do tell us about it."

The little way is the simple way, it is the humble way. It entails that we do every little simple task with deep reverence and devotion and offer it unto the Lord. He who wishes to tread the little way must learn to become humble; in utter surrender he must say to the Lord "Oh Lord, I am nothing! You are everything!"

> This body and soul are Thine
> They are given to me in Thy munificence
> Unto Thee be all the glory
> No stone may tell where I lie!
> May I ever remain nameless!

The words, "No stone may tell where I lie" were very dear to Gurudev Sadhu Vaswani.

Every true saint, every true *bhakta* is aware of this truth; I am nothing, God's grace is everything.

A man of humility is unconcerned about the reaction of other people. He is not hurt by humiliation. He remains calm even when criticised or mocked at. What happens to us when someone criticises, or casts aspersion on us? We get angry. Our immediate reaction is to confront and hit back. Our reaction is to squash the opponent; tit for tat is what we believe in. A single word of criticism ruffles us no end. We do not have the humility to forgive and forget. We do not have the humility to accept the criticism or the harmless joke at our expense. Every single unkind word hurts the ego.

Let us learn to be humble. Let us aspire to the virtue of humility; and let us not commit the fatal error of assuming that we are perfect. If we have even a trace of humility, it is not due to our achievement but thanks to the grace of the Lord.

The light of God shines in all of us, in every creature that breathes the breath of life. But in some of us, the divine light is hidden behind many veils, so that we cannot behold its radiance. These are the veils of pride and ego. When these veils are torn asunder, we can see the divine light shining in all its glory. Humility will surely help us to attain the Lotus Feet of the Lord.

There are three marks of a true friend — If he finds you moving on the path of evil, he will do all he can to set your feet on the path of righteousness. He is not a flatterer: he will tell you the truth even at the cost of incurring your displeasure. And when you are in trouble or in need, he will be the first to rush to your help.

Birds of a Feather Flock Together

Gurudev Sadhu Vaswani, gave this teaching to some of the spiritual aspirants who came to him for blessings and guidance: "Take care of the company you keep!"

Many of you have heard of the proverb which applies this law to our everyday life: "Tell me who your friends are; and I will tell you what kind of a man you are."

This is not mind reading, face reading or occult prophecy; this is basic human and social psychology. Your environment, the company you keep, the people you live with and work with influence your life in more than one way.

We have often seen this in our everyday life. Parents, especially mothers, keep a watchful eye on their children's friends. Some of these friends are invited home so that the mothers may ascertain that they are well-behaved and not undesirable companions to their children.

Businessmen too, are wary of taking on partners; even when the proposed partner is ready to invest a tidy sum of money into the business, they first make sure that he can be trusted, and is not given to cheating or financial misdemeanours.

If such is the case with our worldly relationships, does it not follow that we take care of the company we keep in the pursuit of our spiritual goals? When I say, spiritual goals, I request you not to associate these with renouncing the world! I refer to them as the larger goals, the ultimate goal of fulfillment and liberation that none of us should lose sight of.

Living in the world as we do, our minds cannot remain steady without the protecting influence of *satsang* – fellowship with the pure and holy. Blessed among men is he who lives in fellowship with a saint, a Guru, a realised soul. Such a one helps the seeker to discipline his mind, so that the mind stays calm – even amidst the storms of life.

Gurudev Sadhu Vaswani often said to us, "The law of fellowship is the law of growth. There can be no spiritual growth without fellowship with the pure. Modern life is dominated by economic pursuits: life's daily struggle is deepening: men and women are being increasingly attracted to the material ends of life. It is all the more necessary to have fellowship with some of those to whom the inner values are the true values of life."

Let me give you the words of Kabir:

> Be thou in the company of saints and sages,
> Even if you have to subsist on dry bread crumbs
> For that is better than living a life centred around the self.

Sant Kabir exhorts us to keep the company of the holy ones, even if that means living a life without luxuries and material comforts. He says this is far better than leading a selfish and self-centred life.

Sant Kabir also warns us not to fall into the wrong company under any circumstances – into the hands of bad, unscrupulous individuals, who will mislead us, and distract us from the life of goodness, truth and piety.

Of what earthly use is it if we, the bound souls, keep company with other bound souls? We must seek the company of liberated souls, realised souls, so they can help us to free ourselves!

Unfortunately, such 'bonded' people, not-so-good people, are far more numerous, and far more easily available as friends, than good men, pious men and men of God. In the wrong company, in the company of not-so-good people, the demonic evil that dwells within us is awakened and unleashed, and we lack the strength to conquer our lower self. Only one thing can give us the *shakti* to combat this evil – association with a man of God. The best way to drive out the evil permanently is to awaken within the soul, a deep yearning for the Lord. No matter what hardships we have to bear, we should make it the first and foremost goal of our spiritual life, to find such a holy man, and surrender the thread of our life into his safe hands.

Life is a pilgrimage that we undertake in the company of our fellow human beings. Life means fellowship. This involves building, sustaining and cherishing relationships; it means showing our care and concern for our fellow human beings. But it is equally important that our friendship and fellowship is not frittered away on the wrong people – people who may lead us on the wrong way, and bring about our spiritual degeneration; association with such people should be avoided at all costs.

Friends there may be many, but true friends are few! And a true friend is the greatest blessing in your life – far more valuable than your wealth and possessions; for a true friend is rarer than diamonds and precious stones. All of us like to have such friends. But if you want to have a true friend, you must *be* a friend. Let me quote these famous lines which I have always cherished:

> I went out to find a friend,
> I could not find one there;
> I went out *to be* a friend
> And friends were everywhere!

There are three marks of a true friend:

1. If he finds you moving on the path of evil, he will do all he can to set your feet on the path of righteousness.
2. He will tell you the truth about yourself and the world, even at the cost of incurring your displeasure.
3. When you are in trouble or in need, he will be the first to rush to your help.

When we have to choose our friends and associates, we should be very careful in selecting those who are upright and have moral values. Even more important, we should turn to holy men, men of God, as our Gurus, for at the end of the day it is their pure environment which will take us across the deserts of life.

Who is a man of God? He need not necessarily be one wearing the ochre robes of a *sanyasi*. A holy man is one who is a devotee of the Lord. He is a man of universal vision. He believes all creation is one family and his love is universal.

Unfortunately, many of us are reluctant to choose the company of such a one; for we labour under the wrong notion that it will involve stringent living, a life of austerity and self-discipline. But, as we saw, Sant Kabir in his intuitive wisdom tells us that such a life, a life of simplicity and self-denial is better than being self-centred.

The presence of a holy man works the magic of alchemy on our souls, turning dross material into pure gold. It kindles within us the yearning for God. The very company of a holy man transmits his spiritual fragrance, and the power of his pure vibrations to us. To quote Sant Kabir once again, if you store ordinary logs of firewood with sandalwood, even those common logs of wood become perfumed with the fragrance of sandalwood. Similarly, a piece of iron which is rubbed by the magical *parasmani* (the philosopher's stone) turns into gold. The company of a saint produces a similar effect. Men of the world who live long enough in the company of saints, eventually take to the spiritual path. This is the truth that Sant Kabir conveys to us in his *dohas*. Truly, the influence of a saint can have a miraculous effect on our lives. Living in the company of a saint, you may also become a realised soul one day!

Every human being is different, and has a different aura. Every human being gives out different vibrations. Some vibrations are pure and holy; some are heavy and negative. The pure vibrations uplift you. I am sure many of you must have experienced that with some people you are more comfortable and with others you feel uneasy.

I remember that in the days of my youth, my mother cooked our food on coal fire. Once, she ran out of coal. She asked me to go to a nearby *bazaar* to bring a load of coal immediately. In those days too, as now, I preferred to wear white clothes. I was in the coal shop for some time, arranging for the delivery of the coal with the shopkeeper, fixing the price to be paid, and choosing the right type of coal. When I came out from the shop, I found my white clothes covered with coal dust. Imagine, I had been in the coal shop for under twenty minutes; and my clothes were spotted and stained with black dust.

I am told there is a documentary film, showing how a human child reared by wolves, develops the characteristics of an animal. He walks on all fours and behaves like a sophisticated animal. Of course we all have heard of legendary characters like Tarzan; despite being brought up by wild animals, he has his share of normal human intelligence and skills and an innate sense of culture or civilisation, coupled with a healthy dose of survival instincts; in fact, he seems to have inherited the best of both animal and human worlds and his integration into human society is made to seem relatively easy.

However, reality is very different. I heard from friends about a five-year-old girl, who was found recently in a flat in the Siberian city of Chita, dressed in filthy clothes, barking at people and 'displaying all the attributes of an animal'. This girl, known only as Natasha, had been shut up in a flat for five years with only cats and dogs for company. As a result, she had learnt their behaviour and could not even speak her native language. I am told that she has now been taken into care, but still exhibits dog-like behaviour, preferring to lap her food from a plate rather than using cutlery and jumping up against the door when her carers leave the room. She understands Russian instructions, but can't speak the language, and can only communicate through a series of barks.

Scientists are trying to understand the effects of the environment on the growth and development of children. A lot of questions remain unanswered in this regard. But what I want to emphasise with these examples is the basic fact that the company we keep can influence us for the better or for the worse!

When we move with the people who have good vibrations, we too become attuned to them; we also benefit from their good vibrations.

Hundreds of people come to our *satsang* at the Sadhu Vaswani Mission every day. I am not saying that all of them have become liberated or realised souls! But it is worth asking why they come to our *satsang* day after day. They may or may not be attuned spiritual seekers, but they will tell you that they go there because they receive positive and pure vibrations. They feel comforted. They feel light.

Gurudev Sadhu Vaswani said that people visit sacred places like temples, mosques, churches, holy shrines of saints and sages, and sacred riverbanks, to get benefit of the pure energy there.

Let me add a word of caution; it is true you can pick up positive energy and good vibrations from the *satsang*. But if your efforts are not sustained, you will become equally exposed to the negative vibrations of the world outside!

I recall here a story of a young man who was very regular in our *satsang* in Karachi. He was very fond of our Gurudev Sadhu Vaswani. He was indeed a good man, a pleasant companion to one and all. One fine day, he stopped coming to *satsang*. A few months passed, and I happened to meet him at a friend's place, and I asked him, "How is that I don't see you at *satsang* these days?"

He replied that he had been asked to keep an eye on one of his friends, who had taken to the habit of gambling. "His mother asked me to take care of him; these days I go to the club to keep watch over him. I go there only to stop him from playing high stakes. I am trying to persuade him to give up gambling!"

I was a little taken aback. I said, "What if this works the opposite way? It may happen that he doesn't give up gambling, but you become addicted to the habit – then what?"

He replied: "Don't worry; that will never happen. I am just accompanying him to help him to give up gambling. How will I myself fall a victim to it, when my intentions are clear to me?"

A few more months passed by, and yet, this man did not return to the *satsang*. Later, we found out that he had fallen in the same habit of playing cards at the club. Such is the influence of our friends, neighbours and the people we move around with.

Therefore the wise ones tell us: take care of the company you keep.

The wisdom, knowledge and truth we learn at the Guru's feet cannot be imbibed from books. The Guru provides the Divine spark that can light the flame of transformation within you.

You Can Become New

Have you ever wondered why some people go through constant suffering and misery? Whatever they do, seems to land them in trouble.

It is because they carry the negative vibration pattern of previous births. Such patterns can be changed and transformed only in the company of saints and sages. That is why it is said, in the stormy ocean of life we need the protection and the support of a holy one, who can clear our path and help us move towards more positive, happy and blissful life.

We live at a time when human nature seems to be at its worst. Evil has assumed frightening proportions, and the *vinaasha kaal* (disastrous times) that the holy scriptures speak of, seems close at hand. After all, what is this human nature we speak of? It is but the collective memory of our many previous births, and the residue of indelible *karmic* accumulation. It is very difficult to change human nature. It is next to impossible for us to change our own nature, which is grooved in the past. But what we cannot hope to achieve by our individual effort, a saint's grace can achieve on our behalf.

Gurudev Sadhu Vaswani urged us to be in the company of saints and sages. Saints and sages radiate pure energy. These pure energies are the holy waters of the spirit. They purify and transform all those who come in contact with them. These pure energies can penetrate the subconscious mind and change its set pattern; they can even remove the *vaasanas*, the imprints of previous birth and its *karma*. That is why people seek out saints and sages as to get relief from the negative patterns, which bring sorrow and misery into their life.

Perhaps you do not know that we carry these negative patterns in our subconscious mind from one birth to another. A saint or a holy man can see the root cause of your suffering; a saint can see you suffering. In his company, by his grace, by his blessings, you can purify your past *karmas*, and actually write afresh the script for your destiny.

Once, I accompanied Gurudev Sadhu Vaswani on his visit to Jamshedpur. Here, an ardent admirer and devotee of Gurudev, took us to a beautiful lake. Gurudev Sadhu Vaswani remarked that the environment was beautiful and serene. I thought to myself, "Even in this pure environment there are some people whose minds are disturbed... they lack the spiritual sustenance and nourishment that can give them peace and tranquillity."

Let me tell you, even though our conscious mind may be at rest, our subconscious mind has its own undercurrent of turbulence, and this affects our lives far more powerfully than the workings of the conscious mind! The sub-conscious mind expresses desires of the past through dreams or through psychological compulsions that we don't really understand! This is the reason why good and virtuous people suddenly fall victim to sin. Innocent, smiling people, radiating joy suddenly fall into depression. Sometimes, good leaders commit blunders, which bring them into bad repute. All these negative things happen, even among good people, because of the past *karmas*, and patterns of their desires formed in the subconscious mind. It is only a realised soul, a true Guru who can protect us from the negative influence of these subconscious forces.

Who is a Guru? A Guru is one who has not merely studied the *Vedas* and the Scriptures or one who writes a few books and gives discourses. A Guru is essentially a man of experience, of God-realisation. A true Guru is a friend of God. He walks with God. He talks to God. He lives and moves and has a perpetual fellowship with God. His every moment is spent in the presence of God. There is no difference, no separation, between such a person and God. To see such a one, is to see God Himself. Even if we were to go and meditate in the forest for several years, face hardships and practise austerities, or if we were to undertake a vow of silence or fast for years, or go on pilgrimages; it is nothing compared to spending a short time in the company of a true Guru!

To light a candle, you require another one that is already lit, or a matchstick. Similarly, to be able to kindle the light within, you require the company of a person who is already illumined. The Guru is an illumined soul; it is only he who can help enlighten another soul. That is why we have been told by wise men: seek to find God within you; if you cannot find God, seek out the company of a holy man who has found God within himself!

During my regular morning walks, I noticed a big tree with a huge trunk by the wayside. After a few days the very strong tree had fallen to the ground, uprooted by a cyclonic storm.

The same thing can happen to a man who is strong and virtuous by character; a cyclonic storm of evil desire can devastate him. These desires are often hidden in our subconscious mind, and one doesn't know when and how they will manifest themselves and grab us without a warning. Such sudden storms are difficult to handle. This is why I urge you repeatedly: seek support in *sadh sangat*. The fellowship with the holy ones will give you the strength to face the storm and its turbulence. Alone, you would be destroyed. Being close to a saint, will strengthen you and revitalise your positive energy; it will nullify those uncontrollable, evil desires. The pure and radiant energy you find in the vicinity of a saint will purify you, and protect you!

Man's life is so crowded with mundane activities, that he rarely has time for self-study and introspection. He seldom finds himself in that expansive, tranquil mood of silence and reflection, where he can listen to God, and chant the Name Divine in the heart within.

It is said that the worldly desires are like the salty waters of the sea. Such waters can never quench man's thirst. On the contrary, his thirst increases and his craving for fresh water grows even more acute! To drown yourself wholly in this worldly life is akin to quenching your thirst with salt water.

My humble request to all of you, my fellow pilgrims, is to spare some time for *satsang*. By all means do your work sincerely. Work is essential for a human being. It disciplines his mind and exercises his body. Work is a great boon. But we must remember, work is a means, it is not an end. Livelihood must never be confused with life. Do not make your work the objective of your life on this earth. The purpose of your life is to cultivate the soul. Hence, even while you are attending to your work, stay connected to the Source of all Life; stay in constant touch with God. If you give eight or nine hours a day to your work, it should not be difficult to spare one or two hours to your spiritual growth! This will help you achieve the kind of inner peace and bliss that work can never bring to you.

There is a verse in *Guru Granth Sahib* which tells us, 'Jo Mange Thakur Apnay Te, Soi Soi Devay'. It means – 'Ask and you shall get'. You have to ask Him to shower His Grace on you. Sure enough He will fulfill your request.

Even as you ask for this Grace, make it your practise to seek association with the devout and pious: in other words, start going to *satsang* daily. Participate in *Naam kirtan*. Kindle that flame, which will make you seek the Grace!

Before you begin all else, you must seek the grace of your Guru. The Guru is necessary on this path; without his guidance your progress will be slow. Attain to the Guru's grace: and through the Guru, seek the grace of God! The Guru can certainly show you the path, but the effort must be made by the seeker. First there has to be the 'Intention'; then the quest, and then the Guru's grace, and finally your own effort, which will ultimately bear fruit by the grace of God!

The seeker's path is difficult; the seeker's path is long and weary! We often sing the song in *Satsang* – 'The sea is vast, My boat is frail: I trust in Thee, And all is well!'

We have much to do to reach our goal. We have to face storms. We have to cross treacherous oceans; we have to climb rocky mountains; we have to be tested by fire. It is tough to get past these tests. One thing can get us across safely: The Lord's grace. By His grace alone shall we reach our destination!

Therefore, let us pray to God, 'Be kind, be compassionate, and make me worthy of Thy Grace!'

If we want to be worthy of His kindness, we must be kind to everyone around us. Kindness is a great spiritual quality. Be kind to everyone. Be kind to friends and foes alike. Be kind to birds and animals. Be kind to all people. Do not sit in judgment; do not find fault, do not criticise! Do not gossip. Be kind in thoughts, words and deeds. Kindness brings joy to both – to the one who gives and the one who receives! Seek blessings for all.

A man recently sent me an e-mail. Therein he said, that there was a time when he wept while thinking of God. But today, his emotions have dried up. He was unable to shed tears of longing. "What has become of me?" he questioned, sadly. "How can I recapture the fervour of devotion that I felt for the Lord?"

This man was able to perceive what many of us have failed to take note of. In the quest for worldly wealth, we are losing touch with the higher realities of the spirit. Today, man has become insensitive. He lives a hard, competitive life. He is emotionally dead. Logic and reason have overtaken him and desensitised nay, drained the life out of his feelings and emotions.

Man has to rediscover his heart. He has to reinvest himself with noble sentiments and higher emotions. The highest emotion is love. Let your heart expand and engulf the world with love! That love will bond you with the universe and its Creator.

Guru Nanak has said, the purpose for which you have come can be fulfilled only through your association with saints and sages. Therefore, take the Name Divine with love and hope and devotion. Remember too, that every breath is precious. Our lifespan is predetermined even before we come upon this earth. We have a limited number of days at our disposal. Every person is born with a set number of breaths. We take our breathing for granted, but if you really consider the truth of life, you will come to realise that every breath, every moment, is precious. There is no time to be wasted, for death can knock at our doors any minute!

This human life is precious, but we do not value it.

We count our money; we weigh our position and power most accurately; but alas, we fritter away precious hours and minutes of this rare gift of human birth, without realising their value! We boast that we can earn back the money we lose in the stock market; but have you known anyone who can regain the days he has lost of his life? Can we put back the clock to buy more time from death?

Death, we are told, walks just two steps behind us, though most of us are blissfully unaware of its presence! If you wish to fulfill the purpose of your life before death overtakes you, you must take care of the company you move in. You must seek association with an evolved soul. You must seek the company of good people. The more you move in association of such people, the more goodness will flow into you.

Satsang has a positive effect on man. *Satsang* creates pure and positive vibrations which neutralise the negative emotions of man. When we go to *satsang*, we get to hear discourses of holy men, participate in the recitation of sacred scriptures and singing of soulful *bhajans*. All of this helps to raise the levels of positive vibrations and energises us. For a short time at least, we forget our mundane worries and get immersed in the pure waters of the Spirit. Our emotions rise above the senses, and we cry out, "O Lord! This is bliss. O Lord! You have given me this beautiful gift of life. Till now I have wasted it. But from now onwards, I will strive to achieve the goal of this human birth!"

Some of us are given to reading extensively from the scriptures; some of us perform elaborate rituals of worship; but our minds are not always under our control! Stillness and serenity of the mind is achieved only in fellowship with a saint. He alone has the *shakti* to transform you and make you a new.

You all have your share of worldly friends; keep them by all means; but do not refrain from seeking the fellowship with the holy men, who are friends of God. They are your canopy of protection. Seek shelter under them!

There is the outer silence — it is the absence of noise, freedom from the shouts and tumults of daily life. There is the interior silence — it is freedom from the clamour of conflicting desires. Not until we have this interior silence can we hope to experience unbroken joy.

True Inner Freedom

The other day, I was taking a walk by the seaside with a few friends. The Arabian Sea stretched out before us in a vast blue expanse. The sky was clear and birds were circling overhead. Suddenly we saw a formation, a flock of birds gliding gracefully across the skies. "How I wish I were a bird in the sky," remarked a young girl who was with us.

"You are such a bright young child," I said to her. "Why do you want to be a bird in the sky?"

"I want to be really free, I want to fly," she exclaimed. "Yes, I want to be free as a bird. I want to enjoy the freedom of the open skies."

I was reminded of my own teenage years, when my ambition was to join the Merchant Navy and take to the vast, wide, blue seas!

Every one of us wishes for that kind of freedom. Freedom, which is infinite and limitless!

"My child, if you want to be truly free, then you must know what true freedom is," I said to her. "It is the freedom of the inner self, the freedom you feel from within!"

It is unfortunate, that we look only for outer freedom, whereas true freedom lies within.

As I watched the birds in the sky, I was reminded of the words in that beautiful book, *The Imitation of Christ*.

"If you wish to make progress in virtue, live in the fear of the Lord, do not look for too much freedom," the voice of Christ tells us in this beautiful book. "My child, renounce *self* and you shall find Me. Give up your own self-will, your possessions, and you shall always gain. For once you resign yourself irrevocably, greater grace will be given you..." And again, "If you desire to attain grace and freedom of heart, let the free offering of yourself into the hands of God precede your every action. This is why so few are inwardly free and enlightened — they know not how to renounce themselves entirely."

Isn't that a beautiful thought — to attain inward freedom through utter renunciation? How many of us are capable of giving up something to attain true freedom?

May I ask you, what is your idea of true freedom? Is it to live and act and do whatever you please? Is it to fulfill all your aspirations and desires? Is it to indulge your every whim and fancy? Is it to throw off all restrictions and regulations that keep you chained, confined to a routine that you resent? Or is it something that transcends all this?

The desire to be free, to feel free to pursue one's goals and desires is an innate human aspiration.

Deep within each one of us is an innate desire for freedom. For some of us it is merely felt as a material desire to be free from financial restrictions, to be able to possess whatever we crave for. This may be a new car, a better job or even an expensive holiday abroad. For others, the desire is more mature, more elevated: we wish to achieve true peace, joy, or love. Whether it is freedom from want or freedom from worldly cares, the desire to be free is simply part of human nature.

So what prevents us from achieving this freedom?

We all know of convicts and offenders who are locked in physical prisons behind metal bars under the law of the land; naturally they crave to be released from confinement, to be free like the rest of us. But there is also another confinement that many of us are subject to. I believe that many of us are locked in a mental prison of our own making; we feel restricted, confined, by our own oppressing thoughts and emotions and crave to be free from those crippling negative energies. To be still, to taste that beautiful moment of calm, to feel the central core of peace and bliss that is within, is to be truly happy!

Is it not true that we all long for such moments of absolute freedom, freedom from the demons within?

Remez Sasson, the inspirational writer, tells us that all of us are trapped, imprisoned by the conditioning of our own incessant thinking. Freedom from the compulsion of constant and endless thinking is real freedom.

Our minds are constantly grappling with thoughts from the moment we wake up in the morning until we fall asleep at night. We do not have even a moment's freedom from our thoughts in our waking hours. Thoughts create more thoughts and also receive thoughts from the external world around us. This habit is so strong and deeply embedded that nobody even thinks of overcoming it.

Can you really consider yourself free in such a state? You may be a free citizen living in a free country; you may be financially independent; you may exercise your choice in daily decision making; and yet, and yet, your mind keeps you chained to an incessant flow of thoughts and mental images, many of which are useless and futile and some of which are actually negative and depressing. Outwardly, you are free; but deep within, you are enslaved by your own thought processes.

So ask yourself: what is confining you, restricting you in such a state? It is your own mind. Therefore the Gita tells us: Man is his own friend and man is his own foe. In the measure in which we think good thoughts, positive thoughts, we become our own friends. In the measure in which we think negative thoughts, thoughts of defeat and despair, we become our own foes. Positive thoughts induce magnetism; negative thoughts weaken your magnetism. A cheerful attitude strengthens your magnetism, discouragement weakens it. Hope reinforces your magnetism, despair undermines it. Faith re-emphasises your magnetism, doubt dilutes it. Love empowers your magnetism, hatred takes away from it.

The universe works like an echo: Whatever thoughts you think, will rebound on you. Therefore, be careful of the thoughts you think. Free yourself from the bondage of crippling negative thoughts, before you seek external freedom. Our thoughts are all-powerful. How many of us can really control them?

We must realise once and for all: No one else is to blame for our present condition. We have built it with our own thoughts and desires generated in the near or distant past. Therefore, I tell my friends again and again: "Change your thoughts, and you can change your *karma*. Change your *karma* and you will change the conditions in which you live."

According to Buddhist psychology our consciousness is divided into two parts – very much like a house built on two levels. On the ground floor is the 'living' room, which we may call 'mind-consciousness'. Below this level is a basement, which we can call 'store-consciousness'. Here in this store, all that we have ever said, done, thought, felt and experienced is stored as in an archive. It is as if we sit upstairs in the living room, retrieve from below one DVD after another from the archive, and watch them!

Horror films like *Anger, Fear, Despair*, come up for viewing on their own. They seem to 'pop up' before us whether we want to see them or not. We are forced to spend much of our time watching these films – and they affect our mind-consciousness, our 'living space'. Indeed, I would go so far as to say that they are damaging our lives!

The Gita describes human life as a *kshetra,* an area, a field, where every kind of seed can be planted – seeds of suffering, happiness, anger, pride, joy, peace or sorrow. The store consciousness is also filled with these same seeds. When a thought-seed manifests itself in our minds, we can assume that it returns to the store, stronger than before. We can also assume, that it will return to haunt us again and again. The quality of our life, depends thus on the quality of the seeds we have in store.

Ask yourself – what are the thought-seeds sprouting in your mind? Seeds of anger, sorrow or fear? Or seeds of love, joy, happiness and peace? We must cultivate wholesome seeds consciously. We have to water them, nourish them, and help them grow stronger.

Let me put it another way. Picture yourself standing near your window on a beautiful moonlit night. You look out at the night sky, you are filled with joy and peace and a sense of beauty. You stand there for five minutes, just enjoying the beautiful scene... during those five minutes, you have watered and nourished the seeds of peace, joy and beauty. During those five minutes, seeds of anger, sorrow and despair will not have been watered.

We must cultivate many such moments in our daily life. These seeds of joy and peace that manifest in our mind, grow stronger when they return to the store. These are wholesome, **nutritious seeds, which we must water and cultivate consciously, so that our lives may be filled with peace and healing!**

The trouble with many of us is that we constantly focus our attention on what is wrong with our lives. This is like constantly scratching and re-opening a fresh wound. How will the wound heal if we are constantly prodding and poking at it?

We are sowing seeds every day, every hour, every moment in the field of life. Every thought I think, every word I utter, every deed I perform, every emotion, every feeling, every wish that awakens within me – these are all seeds that I am sowing in the field of my life. In course of time, these seeds will germinate and bear fruit. Bitter or sweet they may be – but I shall have to eat those fruits. No one else can eat them for me.

What you send, comes back to you! Do you gossip about another? You will be gossiped about! Do you send out thoughts of hatred and enmity to another? Hatred and enmity will come back to you, turning your life into a veritable hell!

Do you send out loving thoughts to others? Do you pray for struggling souls? Do you serve those who are in need? Are you kind to passers-by, the pilgrims on the way who seek your hospitality? Then remember, sure as the sun rises in the East, all these things will return to you, making your life beautiful and bright as a rose garden in the season of spring!

You are the architect of your own destiny. You are the builder of your own fate. Every thought, emotion, wish, action, creates *karma*: we have been creating *karma* for millions, perhaps billions of years. If our thoughts, emotions and actions are benevolent, so-called good *karma* results. If they are malevolent, evil or difficult, bad *karma* is created.

When we become aware that our destiny is created by our own thoughts, words, actions and desires, then there is always the possibility that is open to us, to correct and improve ourselves by changing our thoughts and actions for the better!

In this connection, I would like to share with you the Sindhi experience, I may even refer to it as the Sindhi saga of freedom. As many of you know, the Sindhi community is, technically speaking, a stateless community in free India; this is because the land of our birth, the Sindhu *desh*, went wholly into Pakistani territory after Partition. Again, as all of you must know, many of my people came into freedom and independence, walked into independent India, practically penniless, with virtually no possessions except the clothes they carried on their backs!

Today, the (Hindu) Sindhi diaspora is a unique example of a community that was driven away from its native land, became refuges in their own country, and rose like a Phoenix from the smouldering ashes of Partition, to become one of the most successful and philanthropic people in the world. How was this possible? Let me give you the words of Gurudev Sadhu Vaswani:

"...I believe there is a rich treasure in the traditions, folklore and literature of Sind...In the Sindhi soul, there is an immensity, an elemental strength, an aspiration to the Infinite, such as is suggested by the vast deserts of *Sindudesha*... her poets and mystics, her *fakirs* and *dervishes*, her singers and contemplatives, achieved interior freedom... In the simplicity and humanity of her poets and mystics is the seed of a spiritual culture..."

Spiritualism, mysticism, immensity of vision and aspiration to true freedom – the Master has indeed captured the essence of Sindhi literature in a few memorable words!

He would often tell his Sindhi friends that though they had left their lands, their property, their homes and wealth, they had brought with them a far more valuable treasure – the treasure of their culture, traditions and their spirit of freedom!

During the troubled days following the traumatic partition of India, Gurudev Sadhu Vaswani urged the refugees from Sind to be strong within. He exhorted them to be self-sufficient and refrain from begging for government help. Again and again, he repeated those magic words which became a *mantra* of positive thinking for all of us: "Within you lies a hidden *shakti*; awaken that *shakti* and all will be well with you." I remember, too, his unforgettable call to the shattered community, "Believe and achieve."

To believe in ourselves, to believe that we are the architects of our own destiny is true inner freedom!

Selfless service is the bridge that will take you from the life of the world to the life of the spirit.

When Will India be Truly Free

Let me begin with an interesting story about the *Bhagavat Purana*. It is the story of a great king who wanted the ultimate freedom – Liberation – on his own terms!

Long ago there lived a King. A *Pandit* used to go to him every day and read the *Bhagavat* aloud. After every chapter, the *Pandit* would read the closing message, which said: he who religiously reads the *Bhagavat* or hears it, will himself witness the light and will achieve *mukti*, liberation from the cycle of birth and death.

After a few months of daily reading, when the *Pandit* had completed reading the *Bhagavat*, the King asked him a question, "Tell me, have I witnessed the light? Have I reached the stage where I will be released from the cycle of birth and death? Is true Liberation now assured for me?"

To this, the *Pandit* replied, "That is the question which you alone can answer for yourself, your majesty."

The King was not happy with this reply. "You have deceived me," he accused the *Pandit*. "Every evening, I have been hearing the *Bhagavat Purana*. At the end of each chapter you have said to me that he who hears the *Bhagavat Purana* will attain *mukti* and witness the light. Now, you have to prove what you have been reading. I give you one week's time to prove that I have attained liberation. If you fail to prove this, I will send you to the gallows."

The *Pandit* was taken aback. He had expected praise and reward from the King. Instead he had received a threat of death! Depressed, he returned home. Six days passed by, but he could not find any solution to the problem. How was he to prove to the king that after listening to the *Bhagavat Purana*, a man achieves *mukti*? The *Pandit* became worried and despondent.

His seven year old daughter, seeing her father's anguished face, asked him, "Baba, why are your eyes glistening with unbidden tears? What is your problem?"

The *Pandit* opened out his heart to his child. The girl heard him out. Then she said very innocently, "Is that what worries you? Don't cry, for I will come with you to the King's *darbar* tomorrow, and I will explain the situation to the king and hopefully convince him."

On the following day, the girl accompanied the *Pandit* to the King's palace. On entering the *darbar* she ran to one of the ornamental pillars and embraced it. And then, she began to cry at the top of her voice, "O please, please, will someone release me from the grip of this pillar? This pillar is holding me." The King witnessed the scene from his throne and thought that the girl was indeed stupid. Who has brought this foolish child to the court, he wondered. Surely, she was mad. For she herself was clinging to the pillar and shouting to others to come and rescue her!

Aloud, he said to her, "Oh foolish girl, just leave that pillar." The girl cried still louder, "O please, please, separate me from this pillar. Come someone, I have to go back home, but the pillar will not let me go. Have mercy on me and please release me from the clutch of this pillar."

Now the King was really angry. "Who is this stupid girl?" he thundered. "Who has brought her here to my palace? I shall punish them both severely."

On hearing this, the girl left the pillar with a smile. She humbly bowed before the king and said to him, "Your Majesty, you too are holding on to the pillar of your ego. You are unnecessarily blaming my father for not having achieved *mukti*. Leave the ego and you will surely witness the light."

The king realised his mistake. He saw that Liberation is not a gift which someone can present him on a platter. *Mukti* is to be earned. The saints, sages and the scriptures can only show us the path, but it is we who have to walk the path. It is we who have to achieve that inner freedom which is the way to Liberation.

No one will 'grant' you spirituality, no one can present spiritual strength to you. Your spiritual energy has to develop from within. It is you yourself who has to grow and evolve in spiritual strength in order to make a success of your life on earth and in the dimension beyond.

How may we become the masters of our own minds? Through mind control, through meditation, through fellowship, through satsang, through *tapasya*, and symbols and rituals you can achieve your goal. Through the grace of the Guru, all this will detach you from the worldly entanglements; from hurts of broken bonds and lower desires, and then you too, will be free like those birds in the sky.

This inner freedom comes with the adoption of the spiritual ideal.

What is this spiritual ideal? Be desireless, but be duty bound. Remove chains of desires, and be free to fly back to your native home, the Realm of Light! Do your duty by the weaker, the ignorant, the needy, the helpless ones, do so in the awareness that all life is one, and that you are expanding your inner sky in reaching out to these in need of you!

True freedom is of the inner self. True freedom does not mean you break away your bonds with society, your family and move like a vagabond or an aimless tramp. True freedom is not lack of responsibility or accountability.

To be like a bird in the sky is our aspiration. But did you know even birds fly in an orderly formation that enables optimum utilisation of their collective energy and flying abilities? As you may have seen, birds normally fly in what we call a 'V' formation. Do you know why? Have you ever given a thought to it? It has been learned that as each bird flaps its wings, it creates uplift for the bird immediately following. By flying in a 'V' formation, the whole flock adds at least 71% greater range than if each bird flew on its own. Whenever a bird falls out of this formation, it suddenly feels the drag and resistance of trying to go through it alone and quickly gets back into formation to take advantage of the power of the flock.

Science has also discovered that the 'V' formation that migrating birds use serves two important purposes: First, it conserves their energy. Each bird flies slightly above the bird in front of him, resulting in a reduction of wind resistance. Further, the birds take turns being the leader, flying in the front of the formation, and falling back when they get tired. In this way, they can fly for a long time before they stop for rest.

The 'V' formation has this added benefit, that it is easy to keep track of every bird in the group. This is why fighter pilots too use this formation.

The birds in the sky too do their duty – the stronger ones 'facilitate' the weaker ones to move on into the higher regions. Birds do it intuitively; we are rational and emotional beings; we should do it thoughtfully and willingly.

We celebrate 15th August as the Independence Day. India is free. Is India truly free? India may be the largest democracy in the world. Today in 2013, our country presents a perfect secular picture – with a Sikh Prime Minister, a Hindu Brahmin President, a devout Muslim Vice-President, a Dalit as the speaker of Parliament and a Roman Catholic as the leader of the country's ruling party. Despite this noble picture of secularism, India is caught in religious conflict, ethnic violence, and Maoist warfare. Over the last sixty-five years, corruption has increased, greed and selfishness have multiplied, fundamentalism has cascaded, and crime, unemployment have touched new heights.

Today 30% of our people are below the poverty line. And 15% are unemployed and the great dream of an egalitarian, peaceful society is nowhere near realisation.

Can we say India is truly free? No, because its people have fallen victim to selfishness and greed, because its leaders have still to learn, and imbibe the lesson of the birds in flight. Because, they have to care and share, with others!

India will be truly free, when its people will learn to serve their motherland selflessly. They have to be 'facilitators' and not 'grabbers'. They have to be servants of society. They have to be workers and labourers, soldiers, *sipahis* ready to give their all to the welfare of the country and its people.

"What India needs", said, my beloved Gurudev, "is soldiers to work for its peace."

It needs men and women who would be selfless, altruistic, humble, kind and sympathetic. Men and women who would adopt the spiritual ideal of kindness and sympathy!

Every morning in Indian schools, children recite the prayer of unity which begins thus:

India is my country. All Indians are my brothers and sisters.

I love my country and I am proud of its rich and varied heritage.

I shall always strive to be worthy of it.

I shall give my parents, teachers and all elders respect and treat everyone with courtesy.

To my country and my people, I pledge my devotion.

In their well-being and prosperity alone lies my happiness.

How many of us really put into practice this great belief?

How can my country be truly free and prosperous if one fraction of its people live in luxury and opulence while the majority live in poverty and deprivation? Therefore, we must all learn to share what we have with others! Let us set apart a portion — say one-tenth — of our earnings to be utilised in the service of God and His suffering creation.

To some of us, who are unable to make two ends meet, or live within their income, this may at first appear a very difficult thing to do! But we will find eventually, that in the measure in which we share what little we have with others, we will be truly blessed — and this world will be a better place for our humble endeavours!

Most of us are inclined to be self-centered, and to live narrow, selfish lives — but it is only in selfless living that we can discover true inner freedom. And let us not restrict 'giving' to the giving of alms, giving money to the poor! You were surely made for higher things — so give of yourself, give of your time, talents and energies to lighten the loads of the weary and the heavy-laden!

Nowadays, we use the word 'philanthropist' to describe a multi-millionaire who donates vast sums of money to charitable organizations. Many of us do not know that philanthropist is derived from two Greek words, *philas*, which means loving, and *anthropos*, which is man. In other words, the root meaning of philanthropist is a loving man. Aren't we all capable of becoming philanthropists? Of course we are — if we give of ourselves, from a heart filled with love.

In loving and compassionate service, in selfless and caring service lies the secret of a peaceful, united and truly free India!

We regard ourselves as responsible citizens. We pay our taxes and our bills on time; we exercise our franchise and fulfill our democratic duties; we try to obey all traffic rules; we steer clear of breaking the laws of the land; we try not to interfere in other people's affairs . . .

But this is not enough! Doing our duty is alright – but we need to do our duty and a little more! The opposite of love is not hate but indifference, or apathy – apathy to the needs of those around you. We need to contribute our share – our mite – to the welfare of our society, our people, our fellow countrymen. This is what Sri Krishna called *lokasangrha*.

Little drops of water make the mighty ocean! Little grains of sand make this beautiful land. So too, when we all perform little acts of service, little deeds of kindness, the world will be a better place.

Let us turn for inspiration to St. Francis's prayer:

> Lord, make me an instrument of thy Peace,
> Where there is hatred let me sow love,
> Where there is injury, pardon;
> Where there is discord, let me bring truth,
> Where there is doubt, faith;
> Where there is despair, let me bring hope,
> Where there are shadows, may I bring thy Light;
> Where there is sadness, let me bring joy.
> Lord, grant that I may seek rather to comfort than be comforted;
> To understand, than be understood;
> To love, than be loved;
> For it is by giving that one receives,
> It is by forgetting self, that one finds,
> It is by forgiving, that one is forgiven
> It is by dying that one awakens to eternal life.

Conditional love says: - I love you because I need you!
Unconditional loves says: - I need you because I love you!

A Love Story With a Difference

He came here upon this earth long ago! Traditions tell us that Sri Krishna came here 5000 years ago. He came with bewitching beauty. He came with the matchless music of his magical flute. And, even as He played upon the flute, so our *puranas* tell us, even as He played upon the flute, the very winds thrilled, the trees swayed, the rivers resonated, the buzzing bees and the cooing *koel* stopped to listen, and the stars and moon stood still, and hearts were hushed – as divine melody poured forth from the flute!

Who was He? The light of God shone in His eyes, the smile of divinity was on His lips, the wonder of the infinite was in His gaze, and the fragrance of heaven was in His wondrous words.

Who was He? Nameless – for a thousand names are not enough to name Him aright. Who was He? The purest of the pure was He, spotless, stainless; in Him was the light that casts no shadow. Who was He? The *gopas* and the *gopis*, the simple cowherds and milkmaids who had the good fortune to have Him grow up amidst them, whose rare privilege and blessing it was to have beheld His beautiful face, with whom He played games and indulged in a thousand divine *leelas* – the *gopas* and *gopis* exclaimed when they saw Him face to face: "We have seen the light of love in His face! We have seen the rapture of love! We have seen the ecstasy of love! We have seen the face of *ananda* – the bliss that no ending knows!"

One of those fortunate souls was Radha, whose name to this day, is entwined in conjunction with His Divine Name.

Who was Radha? What was she to Krishna that His Name is prefixed by hers, as Radha Krishna! In all our sacred *puranas* the female *Shakti* is given a priority. We have spiritual pairs – Shiv-Paravati, Ram-Sita, and Radha-Krishna.

Why is Radha's name so inextricably linked with Krishna? Radha's birthday is celebrated fifteen days after the *Janmashtami*; it is called Radha *Ashtami*. In north India, Radha *Ashtami* is celebrated with equal zest and enthusiasm as *Janmashtami*, because Radha is considered as the incarnation of Love and Devotion. She is called with reverence- *'Sri Radhey'*, as 'Radha Rani' and 'Radhika'.

For a large number of people in north India, *'Jai Sri Radhey'* is a sacred *mantra*. It is a *mantra*, which leads to the heart of Sri Krishna. People who chant this *mantra* with faith and devotion experience Sri Krishna at a higher level of consciousness. The most ardent devotees of Lord Krishna firmly believe that chanting *'Sri Radhey'* in itself is spiritually beneficial.

My dear brothers and sisters, five thousand years ago came Sri Krishna to reveal the light Divine to the world. He came to show us the true path to Liberation. He was a light unto Himself! He brought the message of freedom from the cycle of birth and death. He, whose goal was to liberate man, Himself took birth in a prison cell, amidst the shackles of thick metal chains. This act is both symbolic and thought provoking. The Lord took birth in the dark and narrow confines of a prison cell so that our souls may witness His Light and be liberated from the prison house of *samsara*!

In the dark hours of the night, soon after His birth, Sri Krishna was secretly taken away to Brindavan. The chains which bound His parents fell away; the prison doors opened on their own; the River Yamuna which was in spate, parted magically to allow the Lord's father to carry His precious child across to Gokul!

In Brindavan, Krishna was the darling of all people. If His foster father and mother adored Him, the *gopas* and *gopis* adored the very ground he walked on!

He stole butter and curds from the *gopis'* houses; but this was not really the crux of the matter. If truth were to be told, He stole something far more valuable; He stole their hearts. That is why we call Him *chitta chora* – stealer of hearts.

There is one Brindavan legend that tells us that Radha was a *gopi* child who was born blind. When Yashoda Ma and Nandagopa walked into the house with their young infant son, it is said that the child Radha, who was one month older than Krishna, stirred and showed signs of animation for the first time since birth; and when her hitherto closed eyes opened for the first time ever, it was Bal Krishna's face that she first beheld – and the rest of her life was Krishna-filled!

The stories of His childhood are immortal. One of the all-time favourites is that one day He played his mischief with the *Gopis*. His mother was so annoyed that she tied Krishna with a rope to a post. (This is why we refer to the Lord lovingly as Damodara – he who was tied with a rope!) The child Krishna in His playful mood dragged the tether, and pulled it to the street to play. At that moment, it is said that Radha happened to be passing by. She was amused by the sight of the determined infant dragging himself on His tether, undeterred by its bonds. She looked at the child Krishna and was totally enchanted with Him!

Even when she moved away, she kept thinking about that wonderful sight, where Krishna's innocence and radiance shone like the brilliant sun. Later on, she came back and followed Him wherever He went. That is why it is said that – if you want to realise Sri Krishna you must take help of Radha – for she knows the path!

Krishna was born at a time when the load of sin was heavy on this earth. The spirit of the earth cried out, "O Lord, I am unable to bear the burden of sin. Please come and free me of this load." It is to redeem the sins of his devotees that Krishna was born. He was the perfect man! He was the perfect incarnation of perfect love! Radha Rani was in search of that love. Radha was restless seeking Krishna. I wish those of you who are reading this will also kindle the same yearning for Krishna as Radha did, so that you too may experience that wonderful energy called love!

The ecstatic *raas leela* of Sri Krishna with the *gopis* – and with His own sweet Radhika – is ever green in the consciousness of the *bhaktas* of the Lord. The unconditional love and absolute devotion of the *gopis* has inspired poets and singers for centuries! As for the love of Radha, it is held up to us as the perfect example of what we call *maadhurya bhava* – the mode of devotion in which the *jivatma* looks up to the *paramatma* as the beloved of the soul!

The scriptural origin of the *raas leela* is to be found in five chapters in Canto X of the *Srimad Bhagavatam*. Known as the *Paanch Adhyaay*, it describes the tricks and pranks of Krishna, who took pleasure in tantalising the *Gopis* with His divine mischief. As we all know, He stole their clothes away and hid them while they were bathing in the river...

When some people read these lyrical passages or see paintings depicting the love-intoxicated *gopis* swooning for the love of Sri Krishna, they frown in disapproval and dismiss the entire *leela* of the Lord as 'erotic' literature. Nothing can be further from the truth! To help you understand the true significance of this immortal *leela*, I take the words of Annie Besant, who captured the very essence of the Lord's *leela*, even though she was a 'foreigner' to our culture and tradition!

This is what Annie Besant has to say on the *Paanch Adhyaay*: "The *Gopis* were *Rishis*, and the Lord Supreme as a babe is teaching them a lesson. But there is more than that. There is a profound occult lesson behind the story. When the Soul is approaching the Supreme Lord at one great stage of initiation, it has to pass through a great ordeal. Stripped of everything on which it has hitherto relied, stripped of everything that is not its inner self, deprived of all external aid, of all external protection, of all external covering, the soul itself, in its own inherent life, must stand alone, with nothing to rely on save the life of the Self within it. If it flinches before the ordeal, if it clings to anything to which it has hitherto looked for help, if in the supreme hour, it cries out for friend or help, the soul fails in that ordeal... alone it must go forth, with absolutely none to aid it save the divinity within itself."

We must realise once and for all that Sri Krishna is no ordinary mortal youth having fun with young ladies! He is the transcendentally Divine Being, the Supreme Brahman who has appeared on earth to uphold *dharma* and offer His protection to *sadhus* and saints who are His devotees.

And in this context, He makes a very important statement which is significant for our understanding of the *Raas Leela*:

> 'In the case of whomsoever that has turned their minds towards Me, the desire or lust that thereby arises in them would not result in anything bad, just as a fried or baked seed would not sprout again'

(X -22 – 26)

How is such a thing possible, that young women could frolic with Him, sing and dance with Him and swoon in His embrace and not be bound by the senses and the passions? King Parikshit, who is listening to the *Bhagavata Purana* asks this question to Sage Shuka. The sage replies:

"The Supreme Lord is inexhaustible and immeasurable, and He is untouched by *Prakriti* because He is its controller. His personal appearance in this world is meant for bestowing the highest benefit on humanity. Persons who constantly direct their lust, anger, fear, protective affection, feeling of impersonal oneness or friendship toward Lord Hari are sure to become absorbed in thought of Him. You should not be so astonished, Oh King, because you are the unique one who had the benefit of seeing His beatific presence even while you were in your mother's womb."

This is the true essence of *Raas Leela*: the union of the *jivatma* with the *paramatman!*

Do you remember the words of that beautiful song:

Kaun kehate hain bhagwaan aate nahin, Radha ki tarah ham bulaate nahin
Kaun kehate hain Bhagwaan naachte nahin, radha ki tarah ham nachaate nahin...

Who is it that can say that Sri Krishna doesn't come to me when I call Him, does not dance for me when I ask Him? Have you called Him with the yearning devotion of Radha? Have you danced with Him in ecstasy as Radha did?

When will we become like Radha, seeking Krishna, and satisfied with nothing else and no one else but Krishna! To seek Krishna we do not need *tapasya* or *yagna* or penance: all we need is the yearning of the heart. And what is the mark of this yearning? The mark of this yearning is tears! Radha's eyes are tear-filled when she returns home after meeting the Lord! Her longing for Him is intense!

What is the ending of this divine love story? Radha, we are told, was the daughter of Vrishabhanu, and was one of the friends of Sri Krishna during that period of His life when He lived among the cowherds of Brindavan. Since childhood they were close to each other – they played, they danced, they fought, they grew up together and wanted to be together forever, but the world pulled them apart. He left *Braja bhoomi* to fulfill the purpose of His *avatara,* namely to destroy evil and protect the good; He departed for Mathura, and she waited for Him. He vanquished His enemies, became the king, and came to be worshipped as a lord of the universe. She waited for Him. He married Rukmini and Satyabhama, raised a family, participated in the great war of Kurukshetra, and she still waited. So great was Radha's love for Krishna that even today her name is uttered whenever Krishna is referred to, and Krishna worship is thought to be incomplete without the deification of Radha.

What is the secret of *bhakti?* What is the attribute of a seeker? A seeker is ever humble. He knows that he is insignificant. That he needs the help of the divine power. Alone by himself he is nothing. He is like a blind man who needs the help of someone to cross the road. He needs God at every moment of his life. Every seeker learns this lesson on the path of self-growth. *Naham naham, tu ho, tu ho!* 'I am nothing O, Lord, Thou art my all!' This Radha knew!

"Deny your self" This is the call of Bhakti. Renounce the ego! Be nothing! Surrender means death of the empirical "I". And when the ego dies man is re-born in the life that is immortal, endless, full of bliss. It is life in Krishna.

The Secret of Radha

Raadhe Krishna! It is said that Radha was given a promise by the Lord that for all time to come, Her name (Radha's) would be taken first before His own (Krishna's) is taken!! Raadhe Krishna!!!

Once we asked Gurudev Sadhu Vaswani: Who was Radha? To this Gurudev replied: Radha is one who has annihilated the ego. And what is the meaning of self-annihilation? Self-annihilation means conquering one's desires! Surrendering oneself totally to a Higher principle!

Commentators of the *Bhagavata Purana* tell us that Krishna's flute is a transcendental symbol of the purest devotion and surrender. We have this lovely legend wherein Radha asks Sri Krishna, "How come the flute is so dear to you? What are its virtues, what is its good *karma* that you hold it close to your lips and allow it to taste the nectar of your breath? And what is my shortcoming that I am always at arm's length from you?"

Sri Krishna replies, "This flute is indeed dear to me. It is close not just to my lips as you say, it is close to my heart because it has become empty, hollowed out its inside and allowed itself to be filled with my music. It has permitted holes to be made on itself, so that it may express my music to the world. It has emptied itself of all egoism, and has become a passage of my breath, an instrument in my hands..."

If we could emulate the flute in this respect, if we could empty ourselves completely of our ego and surrender our wills to the Lord completely, He would produce Divine Music out of our lives too!

An eminent exponent of the *Bhagavat Purana* was once asked why Radha was not mentioned in the *Bhagavat*; he smiled and replied, "If we had to learn all about Sri Radhey and her devotion, we would have to write an entire *Bhagavat* devoted to her!"

There is a beautiful story that tells us of an unforgettable encounter between Radha and Sri Krishna's friend, Uddhava. Uddhava was somewhat embittered and saddened by the fact that he had not been proclaimed a *Maharishi*. In his heart of hearts, he felt that if only his dear friend Krishna put his mind to it, he could indeed become a *Maharishi*. Uddhava even mentioned this to Krishna on a couple of occasions, without eliciting any response from the Lord.

One day, Sri Krishna sent for him and said to him, "I want you to be my emissary and go to Brindaban. When you reach there, you will deliver a special message from me to Radha. Will you do this for me?"

Uddhava knew all about Radha and the pure devotion *prema bhakti* that she had for the Lord. He was overjoyed to think that Sri Krishna had chosen him for such a glorious and deeply personal errand.

Preparations were made for Uddhava's journey from Dwaraka to Brindaban. When Sri Krishna came to bid him goodbye, Uddhava reminded him that he had not yet given the message that he wanted to be delivered to Radha.

Sri Krishna smiled his enchanting smile and said, "That's nothing."

"Nothing?" said Uddhava, puzzled and astonished. "Nothing? Is that why you wanted me to go all the way to Brindaban for? What shall I tell Radha if she asks me for your message?"

"I have given you the message" repeated Krishna. "You can give it to her."

As he drew closer to Brindaban, Uddhava thought that it was very unfair of Krishna to treat Radha with such indifference. He halted his journey and with great effort, he painstakingly composed an epistle of love in extremely flowery language; he decided that he would give it to Radha so that she might not suffer from disappointment.

When he reached Brindaban, he sought out Radha's dwelling and introduced himself. With tear-filled eyes Radha enquired after her beloved Lord. A little awkwardly, Uddhava produced his masterpiece and offered it to Radha as the message from her Lord.

To his surprise, Radha burst out laughing when she read the message! "O, Krishna, Krishna," she exclaimed, wiping tears of mirth and jollity. "He can be so funny!"

"Funny?" stammered Uddhava. "Funny? What do you mean? What does he say in his message?"

"He just says here, 'Uddhava has a lot more to learn before he can become a *Maharishi*'. Isn't that typical of his devious ways?"

Uddhava was stunned. What had become of his imaginative effusions? How did Radha come to know of his ambition? Haltingly, he explained to her that Krishna had given no message for her and that he had written it himself to save her from disappointment.

Radha smiled and said to him, "Where is the need for words between me and the Lord? He is in my heart and soul, and I am an aspect of His Divine Being. I have walked the path of pure love, utmost devotion, complete surrender and silent sacrifice for Him – and He has walked hand in hand with me all the way. Physically he may be far away from me – but every breath I take, every step I walk, every thought I think, thrills with His love! He is with me. I see Him everywhere, in everyone and everything. He does not need to send me any messages. I am His message; my life is His message!"

Uddhava's eyes opened to the truth. He listened speechlessly as Radha explained the deepest mystery of love and devotion to him in crystal clear simplicity. He spent two days at Brindaban and learnt the mystery of true devotion from her.

When he returned to Dwaraka, he was a changed man. Sri Krishna welcomed him back and said to him, "We must now talk seriously about your becoming a *Maharishi*."

"That does not interest me anymore," Uddhava replied.

Sri Krishna embraced him lovingly. "Your learning is now complete. I choose you as the one who will encapsulate my teachings in simple, essential terms and offer them for the benefit of thirsting souls who cannot grasp philosophy."

This was how Sri Krishna's friend became the author of the treatise we call *Uddhava Gita*. Comprising the final teachings of Sri Krishna, this rarely read masterpiece tells us about attaining the highest level of consciousness through devotion and surrender. It emphasises the great truth that Radha revealed to Uddhava – i.e. the importance of seeing Krishna everywhere, in everyone, and at all times.

There are people who question the spirituality of Krishna. There are atheists who put forward arguments denying Sri Krishna's divinity. To many Sri Krishna is no more than a mythological character in the epic of *Mahabharata*. To them I can only say Krishna is not to be read; Krishna is not to be understood with your reason and intellect alone. Krishna is to be experienced! If your heart and soul do not resonate with His awareness, you can never really know him!

Friend of the *Gopas*, Beloved of Brindaban, Disciple of Rishi Sandipani, Astute statesman and Messenger of Peace, Destroyer of countless evil demons, Divine Charioteer for

His friend and Disciple, Arjuna, and the Universal Teacher of *bhakti, karma* and *gnana margas* for all humanity through the Gita – countless are the facets of His Divine personality, and utterly enchanting and inspiring His every word and deed!

Let us confess the truth: is not the very name of Krishna absolutely enchanting! Lord Krishna is love-incarnate. His love extended beyond the playful mischief with *Gopis*. His love was universal. His love went out to cows, birds and other animals. His love went out to those in distress to the sick and the poor and the deprived and the depraved ones! What a mystery was in that immortal love! That is why I said Krishna is to be experienced and not to be debated upon.

I hope you will carry this message with you today. Conquer your desires; overpower them. One by one renounce all the desires. Renounce the desire for higher social status, desire for money power, desire for name and fame! Every one of us has some desire or the other hidden within.

Desires are endless and we waste our whole life in chasing after them. Radha also had a desire, but her desire was for a higher life. She wanted to be with Krishna and only with Krishna. Her desire was more of an aspiration, an insatiable yearning for higher love. This kind of spiritual yearning is born out of the highest order of *bhakti*.

Renunciation of desires does not mean that you do not do your duty. We have to perform our duties. We have to fulfill our responsibilities. We have to live in the world but be not of this world. Living in this world, doing all our allotted duties, we have to have a secret inner life, the life of following Sri Krishna.

The *Paanch adhyaya* gives us this beautiful thought about the Lord:

"The nectar of Your words and the descriptions of Your activities are the life and soul of those suffering in this material world. These narrations, transmitted by learned sages, eradicate one's sinful reactions and bestow good fortune upon whoever hears them. They are filled with spiritual power. Certainly those who spread the message of Godhead must have been munificent..."

Those of you who go to *Satsang* or hear the holy discourses also carry the same yearning within. You only have to be aware of it. You have to intensify your yearning. You have to surrender totally to the Lord with faith, and devotion. Annihilate your desires, and the path will automatically open out to you.

True *bhaktas* of Krishna can never think of the Lord without Radha. Sri Nimbarkacharya give an exalted status to Radha as a manifestation of *bhakti* or *Brahman Vidya* (Knowledge of self) which alone can liberate the *jeeva* from the bondage of *Maya*. It is Radha who becomes the central character in Jayadeva's *Gita Govinda*. Nowhere else will you find so exquisitely rendered, the anguish in separation and joy in union of the divine couple Radha and Krishna. And Radha's love for the Lord is the most supreme form of *bhakti*. Therefore we are told in the *Padma Purana*: "Know Radhika to be best of teachers of the Highest Knowledge — Knowledge of Brahman."

When Sri Chaitanya Mahaprabhu took birth amongst us, he chose the immortal *leela* of Krishna to spread the power of chanting and singing the Name Divine. He tells us: "A devotee should be humble, forgiving, forbearing, respecting to the devotional feelings of others, but not desiring for any personal compliments for himself. With such a humble heart, which is yearning for the vision and association of his beloved Krishna, the devotee should sing and chant the *leelas* and the names of Krishna." Are these not the attributes of Radha?

The eternal *leela* of Radha and Krishna is the ultimate experience of *brahma sukha anubhava* — spiritual pleasure of union with the Lord, pleasure of the highest order! All of us crave for *sukha* or pleasure, but we allow our pleasure to be contaminated by material desires!

Radha was the most beautiful, the most devoted and the most beloved of all *gopis*! The *raas leela* of Radha and Krishna is not just a dance or a pleasurable interlude of fun; it is symbolic of the eternal love affair between the devoted mortal soul, the *jivatma* and the Supreme Divine Being, the *Paramatman*. The *jivatma* is caught up in our mortal coils; but it never ceases to yearn for union with the Divine. That is why all true *bhaktas* are regarded as women, while He alone is the One without a second. Thus Radha's yearning for her beloved Krishna is nothing but the soul's longing for spiritual awakening – to be united with the one Source of Peace and Bliss from which it has become separated.

To those of you who still keep wondering, "Why is it that Sri Krishna married Rukmini and not Radha?" here is my answer: Radha had already internalised Krishna within her; she had conquered all outward desires and only allowed the inward flow of Krishna consciousness. In short, she was one with Sri Krishna. They were inseparable in spirit!

All of us are in search of peace and happiness; in our state of *maya* and *avidya*, we seek them through sense objects. But when we turn our hearts to God in loving devotion, we experience the bliss, the joy and the peace that no ending knows! As the Lord says in the *Srimad Bhagavatam*, "The mind that constantly contemplates upon the sense objects, irresistibly comes to revel in their finite joys, and the mind that learns to constantly remember Me comes to dissolve into Me." It is this state of pure devotion that Radha represents!

In sheer agony of the heart, a man cried: - "My sins are greater than the mountains. What shall I do?" and he heard a voice which said:- "Only love Me — and all thy sins will be washed away!"

Ten Types of Sin

Shrimad Bhagavata Purana opens with these words:

> *Once, in a holy place in the forest of Naimisharanya, great sages headed by the sage Saunaka assembled to perform a great thousand-year sacrifice for the satisfaction of the Lord and His devotees...*

It was the last phase of the *Dwapara Yuga*: the *Kaliyuga* was about to begin. In ancient India, our great sages were always anxious to do good to the people, to bring about real peace and prosperity to the land. The sages thus engaged in performing the *yagna*, enquired of their leader, Ugrasrava, also known as Maharishi Suta Goswami, as to how the people living in the dreaded *Kaliyuga* may protect themselves from its evil effects.

They said to him, "In this dark age of Kali, men have but short lives. They are quarrelsome, lazy, misguided, unlucky and, above all, always disturbed. They do not know how to live spiritually vibrant lives. Obsessed as they are with comforts and luxuries, people will find it difficult to practise *tapasya* (austerity), read the scriptures or perform *yagnas* (sacrifices). Men will be preoccupied with their work, their business, their calculations of profit and loss. They will be slaves of unholy desires: they will experience strain and stress; their lives will be filled with tension, worry and anxiety. They will have neither time nor inclination to follow spiritual pursuits. Under these circumstances how will dormant souls wake up and draw closer to God? How can the people find happiness on earth? How can they find salvation?"

In answer the Blessed One said, "What you say is true. The condition of humanity will indeed be pitiable in *kaliyuga*. Their lives will be steeped in sin. They will live in fear of death."

There are ten kinds of sins, which people are prone to fall into, in this dark age of *kali*. What are they?

Let me begin by saying that Hinduism views sin and evil from the perspective of the profound philosophy of *karma*. All of us are free agents and we generate our future destiny by the consequences of our own actions, words and thoughts. The choice is ours: when we choose good over evil, good *karma* results; when we choose wrong over right, bad *karma* results. Unlike other religions, 'sin' is not an act of willful rebellion against God in the Hindu way of life: human beings are not born with sin, nor do they become sinners damned forever by their actions. Rather, they choose the wrong way as a consequence of their *karma*, and thus reap unhappiness. As you sow, so you reap, is the essence of Hindu philosophy. As a wise man once said to me, "We are not punished for our sins, but by our sins." We use the English word 'sin' because it is a convenient term, but the connotations for Hindu philosophy are quite different. Let us bear this in mind, as we continue with the evil that man falls into, through wrong choices.

India's distinguished philosopher-statesman, Dr. Radhakrishnan, expresses this truth admirably when he says: "The cards in the game of life are given to us, we do not select them. They are traced to our past *karma*, but we can call as we please, lead what suit we will, and as we play, we gain or lose. And there is freedom." Therefore our spiritual masters urge us to be very careful about our thoughts, because thoughts create, and thoughts also make *karmas*, good, bad and mixed.

Of the ten types of 'sins' I spoke of, three types are the products of the mind; four are the result of our speech; and the remaining three evils are associated with the physical body.

Our scriptures therefore tell us:

> Action, which springs from the mind, from speech, and from the body, produces either good or evil results.

The mind is the instigator of action which is connected with the body and which is of three kinds, has three locations, and falls under ten heads.

Coveting the property of others, thinking in one's heart of what is undesirable, and adherence to false doctrines, are the three kinds of sinful mental action.

Abusing others, speaking untruth, detracting from the merits of all men, and talking idly, are the four kinds of evil verbal action.

Taking away by violence that which does not belong to us; injuring other creatures wantonly; and holding illicit physical relations with another are declared to be the three kinds of evil bodily action.

What are those sins caused by the mind?

The first sin is one which we keep on committing over and over again, without even being aware of it! For some of us, it is a sin we fall prey to, every thinking minute of the day! This sin is committed when we harbour an evil thought about another person. Surprisingly, many of us do not consider this as a sin. We feel that these thoughts are confined to the mind and no one knows about them. "I've not actually DONE anything or even said anything," we rationalise. "It's only a thought."

I have said this to my friends over and over again: thoughts are forces; thoughts have power; thoughts determine our *karma* – for every thought we think is a seed we sow in the field of our life. Thoughts of vengeance create ill feelings;

thoughts of blame and criticism bring negativity back to us; thoughts of anger and resentment poison our goodwill. When we think of harming others, hurting them, or insulting them, we are sowing seeds of bitter fruits in our minds. These thoughts may be invisible to others; but sooner or later they take shape as actions. The pent-up negativity and anger will find expression outwardly; or worse still, they will begin to fester inside us, poisoning our minds and hearts. Although no one sees these thoughts and feelings, they send out negative vibrations; which though unseen, reach the person for whom they are intended, and invariably reverberate on us. Let us be aware and alert: every evil thought which arises in the mind is a sin.

I am sorry to say that some of us even harbour evil thoughts against the Guru! We do not go to the Guru in the spirit of true obedience and reverence. We expect the Guru to pay all his attention to us, approve of our every word and action, appreciate all that we do and shower praise on us. When this does not happen, when the Guru is busy with others, or praises someone whom we don't like, we are quick to take offence; we think ill of him; we say to ourselves: "Ah, my Guru is taken in, deceived by so-and-so; he doesn't realise the truth..." and so on and so forth! A few people, in such a bitter mood, even compare their own Guru unfavourably with other spiritual leaders. "Such and such a *swamiji* is far more profound..." they say to their friends. "I don't think our Guru is so clear about this point." Why, I have even heard some people remark, "Our Guru gets carried away too easily. So-and-so is far more perceptive."

Who are we that we set ourselves up in judgment against the Guru? How can we even imagine that the Guru has to please us in everything he says and does? We are looking for foolish flattery, not guidance and good counsel!

The Gaudia Vaishnavite tradition tells us: "Never look upon Sri Guru as a worldly man and never lend your ears to

Guru-ninda. (slander against the Guru). Never even look in the face of them that speak ill of the Guru and avoid the place where *Guru-ninda* is heard."

Sometimes, our envy and jealousy blind us to such an extent, that we even wish that the Guru would fall ill or be punished in some way!

Once I met a man who was full of remorse. He said to me, "All kinds of evil thoughts come to my mind. But worst of all are those unforgivable, evil thoughts against my Guru. Today I went to my Guru. He did not pay any attention to me. He did not acknowledge my presence. He did not even give me a glance. He totally ignored me. This angered me. On the way I saw a banana skin and I wished that my Guru would walk on it and slip over it. In my anger I wished that he may break his leg."

Having confessed this, the man burst out into tears because he was overwhelmed by his own arrogance and guilt: guilty for entertaining such evil thoughts about his Guru whom he loved and revered. And yet he could not help thinking such thoughts! That is the power of the sin of the mind. We cannot control them. Such thoughts obviously are sinful.

Such thoughts only weaken the mind. We lose energy in such worthless negative thoughts. Man should be the master of his mind. But today the mind has become the master of man. Control the mind, and overcome this first sin.

The second sin of the mind is when we indulge in thoughts of lust. Again, we console ourselves with the thought that we have not done anything; but the evil has already germinated in the mind! Whether you satisfy your sexual urges or not, the very thought of lust is sinful. Hence, learn to think pure thoughts.

The third sin of the mind is manipulation of the truth. Very often the mind justifies the actions by manipulating the meaning of the sacred words of the scripture to its advantage.

A case in point is the Lord's injunction to us in the Gita: the famous lines which begin: *Sarva dharman paritajya maamekam sharanam vraja*... Renouncing all rites and writ duties come to Me for refuge... How we love to manipulate those words!

In this special promise to us, the Lord takes all responsibility for one who surrenders unto Him, and He assures us that such a person will be protected against all reactions of sins. But some of us deliberately misinterpret these words to suit our convenience: I know of foolish husbands, fathers and sons who ran away from their family responsibilities to take *sanyasa*, under the pretext that they were renouncing their bounden duties to surrender to the Lord. That is NOT what the Lord meant when He tells us to renounce writ duties! He asks us to surrender the fruits of our actions unto Him; He urges us to surrender the thread of life into His capable hands and dedicate all our actions to Him!

Sometimes even ardent disciples twist and turn the words of their Master to suit their selfish purpose. As Srila Prabhupada tells us, "He who remains a great fool before his Guru is a Guru himself. However, if one thinks, 'I am so advanced that I can speak better than my Guru,' he is simply a rascal."

Thus: thinking evil thoughts about others; indulging in thoughts of lust; and manipulation of the truth are the three sins which are the work of the mind.

The four sins committed by speech are – Speaking lies, being judgemental or criticising others, harsh angry words; and idle talk.

Perhaps we do not realise that we have formed the habit of speaking untruth. Every day we speak lies because our conscience is not awakened. Our conscience is sleeping; hence, we speak lies without even being aware of it, leave alone feeling guilty about it. Thus, everyday, we utter falsehoods blithely, to protect ourselves, to please others, or just to escape from tricky situations. But we would do well to remember the beautiful words of the *bhajan* that was so dear to Gandhiji: *Jihvaa thaki asatya na bole...* His tongue would fail him if he attempted to speak an untruth. Even such a one is a true devotee of the Lord.

Let your conscience be awakened. Be alert, speak the truth, and do not commit the sin of uttering falsehood!

The second sin committed by speech is criticising others and denigrating them. Nowadays, when friends meet they do not talk of *satsang* or God; they discuss other people, often criticising them or speaking ill of them.

The great Prophet of the Baha'i faith, Baha'ullah, said to his disciples, again and again, "If you find that there are nine vices and only one virtue in your neighbour, forget the nine vices, and focus only on the one virtue."

This is the secret of an understanding heart. See only the good in others. When we focus on others' faults, we only draw those negative forces unto ourselves. Fault-finding, constant criticism and magnifying the mistakes of others are poor, ineffective ways of changing the world.

Try a smile or a kind word – you will find that wrongs are easy to set right, and 'wrong doers' are set back on the right track!

Repetition of God's Name is the most effective remedy for all the ills of life. It is a potent pep-pill that will lift you out of depression and exhaustion.

The Easiest Way to God in Kaliyuga

We were talking of three kinds of sins: sins of thought, speech and body.

A young spiritual aspirant grew so much in the love of God, that she was actually able to commune with Sri Krishna, her *ishta devata*. A doubting, faithless priest wished to put her to the test. "If, as you claim, you really commune with Sri Krishna every day, ask Him to tell you what was the sin I committed when I was a young man."

He was sure that she would never find out. And this would expose her claim as being false.

Next week, he sought her out and asked her, "Have you spoken to Sri Krishna?"

"Yes, I did," she replied.

"And did He tell you what was the sin I committed?"

"He said that He had forgotten it – and wanted you to do the same."

The doubting priest hung his head in shame.

If God does not keep a tally of people's faults and failings, why should we? And are we so perfect that we can go on counting, enumerating and elaborating on the faults of another?

The third sin committed by speech is harsh words. Whenever we speak harsh words, we become a party to causing hurt and pain to another. Harsh, angry words can ruin a life. I always say to my friends: of the unspoken words, you are the Master; of the spoken word, you are the slave.

God has given us the faculty of speech to utter sweet, kind and gentle words. God has given us this tongue to utter words of comfort, hope and healing to those who need them. As the Book of Proverbs tells us, "Kind words are like honey — sweet to the soul and healthy for the body."

Speak sweetly and gently with all. And to everyone who meets you pass on the sunbeams of your smile and the loving service you render will be to you as music at mid night.

Let me tell you those lines which I have always been thrilled to hear:

> Speak gently,
> Walk humbly,
> Give something in charity.
> Then you need not to the forest go,
> For the Lord is with you already!

A veritable roadmap for the Life Beautiful is given us in those three injunctions: (1) Speak sweetly (2) Walk humbly and (3) Give something in charity with your own hands.

The fourth sin of speech is idle talk or gossip. Gossip is unnecessary and does no good to anyone. We waste our time and our precious energy in gossiping about others. By this we gain nothing and lose a lot.

Gurudev Sadhu Vaswani always said to us, "Keep your distance from the world and worldly affairs. Keep yourself away from people who indulge in malicious gossip. Speak less, because if you speak much, you are likely to utter a lie or two. Keep your talk restricted to the minimum. If you want to talk more, then talk about good things, about God and His nature, His creation and His universe. Alternatively, simply chant the Name Divine: *Rama gun gana, Hari gun gana.*"

It is human nature to exaggerate the faults and weaknesses of others, and to pretend that we ourselves are faultless. Hence, we should control our speech and talk less. Always speak the truth and earn the rich blessings of the Lord and the Guru.

Gurudev Sadhu Vaswani gave great importance to the virtue of honesty. He urged us to be truthful and honest in all our dealings. His emphasis was on earning the rich treasures of the spirit, rather than the material things of this world.

I remember, a few days before Gurudev Sadhu Vaswani dropped his body and merged with the Infinite, a girl from abroad had visited him. She asked for a message; Gurudev Sadhu Vaswani said, "Bear witness to the truth, always speak the truth and you will soon realise God."

In ancient India, truth was a way of life. There is a song which tells us: There is nothing greater than the truth. All falsehood is a sin. God resides in the hearts of those who bear witness to the truth. There was a time when India was known for her radiant culture, the Culture of Light and Truth. The very word *Indian* meant the truthful one. India was known for her spiritual qualities and values. Alas, today things are very different. Today India is being described in negative terms and being degraded. India has yielded to corrupt practices, exploitations and falsehood of misguided men. Truth seems to have disappeared from our lives.

When Mahatma Gandhi was a student, a question was put to him, "What is more precious than gold?" Mahatma Gandhi replied, "Truth is more precious than gold and there is nothing more precious than Truth."

How I wish we may imbibe the value of truth in our daily lives!

In ancient India, it was said, "Learn the lesson of truth, even if the teacher of that lesson is not truthful." Your duty is to imbibe the truth and not to judge the dispenser of the truth. Truth even from a sinner is truth. It is invaluable. Accept the truth and overlook everything else.

In this *kaliyuga* — the age of evil — the easiest *sadhana* is to be truthful. The important message of the *rishis* and the saints is: Be honest and bear witness to the truth.

Sant Tulsidas, in his sacred book, *Sri Ram Charitra Manas*, says: "If you speak the truth, if you consider every woman as your mother, then you can realise God. If you do not realise God, by adopting these two principles, then you can consider me as a hypocrite."

Let us realise therefore, that truth is the core of all religious teachings. For, God is Truth Incarnate, all else is an illusion. I humbly request you to be honest, sincere and bear witness to the gospel of truth. Make truth the anchor of your life and be richly blessed!

Falsehood, denigration of others, harsh words and idle talk then, are the four sins of speech.

Three sins are associated with the physical body. They are physical violence, sexual abuse and theft.

The first sin committed by the body is '*Hinsa*', physical violence. We would do well to remember that physical violence means not only murder of human beings, but also the senseless slaughter of other living creatures that breathe the breath of life; animals have no courts to appeal to, in fact they even lack a voice to plead for mercy. I am afraid that physical violence towards man and animals is all too common these days. It is rampant throughout the world. Slapping a child, hitting a wife, son, or daughter or daughter-in-law is also violence. Killing an animal for food, to please our palate is also a sin of violence. We all are perpetrators of such violence in our daily living.

The second type of physical violence committed is 'rape' or 'sexual abuse'. I am truly horrified by the frequency with which this evil occurs in our society, day after day.

The third type of violence committed by the physical body is stealing or 'theft'. Forcibly taking away from others what does not belong to us; snatching away someone's property; cheating others for a little gain, or using force for one's own benefit, are all forms of theft. Indulging in corruption, misuse of public property and public funds is also a form of theft.

We have discussed ten different types of sins. If we examine our own lives carefully, we will have to admit that each one of us commits one or more of these sins every day. The burden increases till Mother Earth finds it impossible to carry the load of our accumulated sins. In this *Kaliyuga* man is deep into sinning. In the *Kaliyuga,* man has become a pleasure hunter, a proud egoist and a selfish being.

But to return to our story: This was the issue taken up at the gathering of the sages in *Naimisharanya kshetra*. If this was the situation, then how can men seek to attain the Lotus Feet of the Lord? Is it possible to live the life beautiful? The *Rishis* debated this question and sought guidance from the enlightened one who had studied at the feet of *Rishi* Ved Vyas.

The enlightened one said: "In the *Kaliyuga* where man lives in utter spiritual darkness, there is only one simple solution available to this problem. It is *kirtan, naam simran* – chanting the name divine."

There are various spiritual *sadhanas,* various techniques of spiritual growth recommended for different world ages. Thus *tapasya* and *yajna* were the accepted practices for spiritual development in the era when the Lord walked upon this earth as Sri Rama and Sri Krishna. We learn from the Gita that even Arjuna, Lord Krishna's close friend and dear disciple, found some of these techniques daunting. Having heard from the Lord about the technique of *dhyana* or meditation, Arjuna remarks that the fickle, turbulent, strong and obstinate mind is very difficult to control. How then, can we attain to the *yoga* of equanimity? And what of the man who strives, but does not succeed?

The Lord assures him that no man who is a sincere seeker can come to an evil end. Our striving, our efforts at self-realisation will eventually help us. We need never despair, for the Lord is all love and compassion, and will not let our sincere efforts go in vain. We will rise, step by step, to realisation.

Thus the Gita holds out to every seeker the hope, nay, the promise, that though he falls a hundred times, he will rise again! His failures are only temporary.

The *tapasvi* (ascetic) inflicts severe penances on his body; the *gnani* (knower of the Vedas) is learned and wise; the *karmi* (man of activity) is hard working and sincere. But greater than them all is the true *yogi*. And the best of *yogis*, according to the Gita, is he who offers to the Lord his love and devotion, and worships Him in faith.

> And, of all *yogis*, he who, full of faith adoreth Me, with his Self abiding in Me, he is deemed by Me to be the most completely harmonised (the most devoted).
>
> [VI:47]

Chanting the Name Divine is the surest, easiest way to become completely harmonised in the Lord! It achieves the impossible, by keeping all our senses under control! We are singing or chanting; we are listening to others chanting around us; our hands are folded together in tribute, or we are clapping gently in rhythm with the chanting; we keep our eyes closed in the involvement of the *kirtan*; or we are gazing at the radiant face of the Guru or focusing on the image of our *ishta devata*; the tongue is tasting the nectar of the Name Divine; the smell of incense and *agarbattis* fills the air; it is a feast divine for all the senses!

A western scholar of Hindu beliefs and practices actually describes this as *kirtan yoga!* It is easy, simple and practical; all of us can practise it effortlessly!

Chanting in groups is particularly beneficial. It cleanses and heals body, mind and soul. It clears your aura. It paves the way for the Life Beautiful! Therefore, let us all chant and sing the Name Divine – not mechanically, but with love and devotion!

There are two types of *'Kirtan'*. One, in which you simply chant the Name Divine; the other in describing and singing His glories. The first type of *kirtan* is what you do for a few minutes in *satsang*. *Kirtan* should not be limited to time. It should not be bound by the minutes and hours. *Kirtan* should be continuous; it should bring joy and ecstasy to the group chanting. *Kirtan* is spiritually intoxicating! When continued for a long time, it spreads its beautiful, peaceful vibrations and uplifts the soul!

The second type of *kirtan* is singing the glories of the Lord, such as describing the *'leela'* of Krishna in Brindaban! His miraculous birth, His *raas leela* with the *gopis*; His living with cowherds; His tantalising ways! Singing those glories of the Lord or even thinking about Him is also a form of *kirtan*!

For *kirtan* only one thing is absolutely essential: devotion for the Lord and yearning for His Lotus Feet. Devotion comes with faith. Devotion or *Bhakti* is an emotional upsurge. It powers us from within. It comes with a certain conviction. The chant by itself or singing by itself does not purify you. It is your *bhava* – Your emotion which will release the subtle forces of cleansing that will purify your inner instrument and elevate your soul to sublime heights of *bhakti*. Ultimately it is your intense devotion which will kindle the yearning for the Lord. This is the beginning of true transformation. This is when you see the spark of divine light which dispels the darkness of the *Kaliyuga* that is enveloping you on the outside.

Kirtan is *'Sahaj Marg'* – it is an easy path. You can do *kirtan* anywhere, anytime of the day. You can think of the life of great ones, anywhere and anytime of the day. The beautiful thoughts about the Radiant Ones will purify your interior and a day will come when you will behold, the golden light within!